Fifth Edition

Information Literacy
& *Technology*

Carla List-Handley
Holly Heller-Ross
Elin O'Hara-Gonya
Alison Armstrong

Kendall Hunt
publishing company

Book Team

Chairman and Chief Executive Officer   Mark C. Falb
President and Chief Operating Officer   Chad M. Chandlee
Vice President, Higher Education   David L. Tart
Senior Managing Editor   Ray Wood
Assistant Editor   Bob Largent
Vice President, Operations   Timothy J. Beitzel
Assistant Vice President, Production Services   Christine E. O'Brien
Project Coordinator   Traci Vaske
Permissions Editor   Tammy Hunt
Cover Designer   Jenifer Fensterman

Author photos courtesy of Mark Mastrean

Cover images © Shutterstock, Inc.

Kendall Hunt
publishing company

Swww.kendallhunt.com
Send all inquiries to:
4050 Westmark Drive
Dubuque, IA 52004-1840

Copyright © 1998, 2002, 2005, 2008, and 2013 by Kendall Hunt Publishing Company

ISBN 978-1-4652-0482-0

Printed in the United States of America

10   9   8   7   6   5   4   3   2

Contents

Author Biographical Info

Carla List-Handley taught information research to undergraduates at SUNY Plattsburgh for more than 20 years. She received her Master of Arts in Library Science from the University of Iowa. She received the State University of New York Chancellor's Award for Excellence in Librarianship in 1995, and was named the Librarian of the Year in 1997 by the Eastern New York Chapter of the Association of College and Research Libraries. She was promoted to SUNY Distinguished Librarian in 2003.

Alison Armstrong is the Director of Information & Instruction Services at the University of Vermont. Prior to that, she worked as the Director of Undergraduate Initiatives and Head of the College Library at UCLA. Alison has also held various positions at the American University in Cairo (AUC), the University of Cincinnati and at the University of Nevada, Las Vegas. She earned a Master of Arts in Library Studies and a Bachelor of Arts in English from the University of Wisconsin, Madison. Alison's work has focused on undergraduate library services related to teaching, learning, and technology and she has spoken and published on topics related to information literacy and student learning, including critical thinking, research skills, and the role of technology

Holly Heller-Ross is Dean of Library & Information Services at SUNY Plattsburgh. She has a B.A. in Environmental Science from Plattsburgh and an MLS from SUNY Albany. She worked as a public librarian and then hospital librarian before joining the faculty at Plattsburgh in 1994. Holly attended the ACRL Institute for Information Literacy Immersion programs in 1999 and 2002. She received the SUNY Chancellors Award for Excellence in Librarianship in 2000, was a 2003 Fellow in the Plattsburgh State University Institute for Ethics in Public Life, and conducted research in Cairo, Egypt as a Fulbright Scholar, studying information literacy and librarianship at the University of Cairo in 2007.

Elin O'Hara-Gonya is an Instruction & Reference Librarian at the SUNY Plattsburgh. She earned her Master of Library Science from Southern Connecticut State University and a Bachelor of Arts in International Studies from American University. She will earn a Master of Science in Mental Health Counseling from the State University of New York College at Plattsburgh in 2013. Elin's research has focused on undergraduate information literacy topics, as well as the effects of student emotional problems on the practice of reference librarianship.

Introduction to the Fifth Edition

■ ■ ■

"The illiterate of the 21st century will not be those who cannot read and write, but those who cannot learn, unlearn, and relearn."

—ALVIN TOFFLER *FUTURE SHOCK,* 1970

On most campuses in the United States, the phrase "information literacy" has replaced "information research" as a goal for those who educate college students. What's the difference between information literacy and information research? The newer term is more comprehensive than the old one.

The American Library Association's definition of an information literate citizen is one who is "able to recognize when information is needed and have the ability to locate, evaluate, and use effectively the needed information." Courses now strive to teach students good information research skills and understanding along with explanations, discussion of, and practice at *using* information ethically. Many courses also include work with various information technologies, from word processing to webpage construction.

Understanding the systems that are used to organize information is still the best way to ground oneself in the use of information technology and in doing information research. This book still discusses those systems. The 4th edition expanded the more complex idea of information literacy whereas this 5th edition focuses primarily on the components of information literacy that are involved in information research. And because information research is never a strictly linear activity, the chapters have been rearranged to try to reflect that.

One course will never create "the information literate student." Rather, using information, finding information, and creating information in *all* the courses in your college career will contribute to your information literacy, your continual learning to learn, and your ability to "unlearn, and relearn" for the rest of your life.

Carla List-Handley, May 28, 2012

■ ■ ■

". . . overload 'em with information and they'll kill ya just to simplify things."

—RUBEUS HAGRID, IN *HARRY POTTER AND THE ORDER OF THE PHOENIX*

How to Use This Book

This edition—

- Explains the basic systems used to organize information
- Helps readers clearly define their information needs
- Addresses concepts and skills that are foundational to information literacy
- Identifies issues and questions of appropriate and ethical use of information

Features include:

- Learning objectives at the beginning of each chapter
- Chapter highlights at the end of each chapter
- Search Tips and Concept Checks that emphasize important concepts and provide opportunities for further clarity
- Skill Checks that provide opportunity for students to apply concepts as they learn them
- Screenshots throughout the text to help readers visualize textual concepts and skills
- Suggested assignment questions for each chapter with additional assignments on the companion website
- A Comprehensive research assignment on the companion website
- A Glossary that defines important information and technology literacy research terms
- A Bibliography that cites sources quoted in the text and provides a model for readers

■ ■ ■

"Research is formalized curiosity. It is poking and prying with a purpose. It is a seeking that he who wishes may know the cosmic secrets of the world and they that dwell therein."

—ZORA NEALE HURSTON *DUST TRACKS ON A ROAD,* 1942

Planning

LEARNING OBJECTIVES

- Begin to understand how information is organized and disseminated
- Identify the value and differences of potential resources in a variety of formats
- Describe a general process for searching for information
- Describe when different types of information (e.g., primary/secondary, background/specific) may be suitable for different purposes
- Define and Articulate the need for information

Information is everywhere and in great quantity. How can you deal with the vast amounts you encounter? How can you best plan your research, analyze your topic, and become information literate? You can begin by understanding what information is and how you can organize it.

WHAT IS INFORMATION?

One definition of the word information comes from International Federation of Library Associations and Institutions (IFLA, 1999) "all ideas, facts, and imaginative works of the mind which have been communicated, recorded, published and/or distributed formally or informally in any format." This means that information can be a fact that was recorded by a person using a stylus to etch it on a stone tablet, a folk tale that was handed down orally for many generations, an images-only comic book that was printed and distributed to thousands of readers, or an idea that was communicated electronically through computers or television.

WHY IS IT NECESSARY TO ORGANIZE INFORMATION?

Organization of information makes it manageable and helps you handle it rather than being overwhelmed by it. If there were no access to the vast amount of information that is available there might as well be no information. How does organization improve access to information? Organization is the arrangement of items into a system. A system establishes rules, or reasons for arranging items in certain ways, and then applies them consistently to the materials it organizes. In a good system the reasons that form the basis for the system remain the same throughout and are readily apparent, intuitive or easily learned. Thus you, as a user of a system, can be confident that the way you learned how to find items one time in a particular system will work a second time, a third time, and so on. You might be

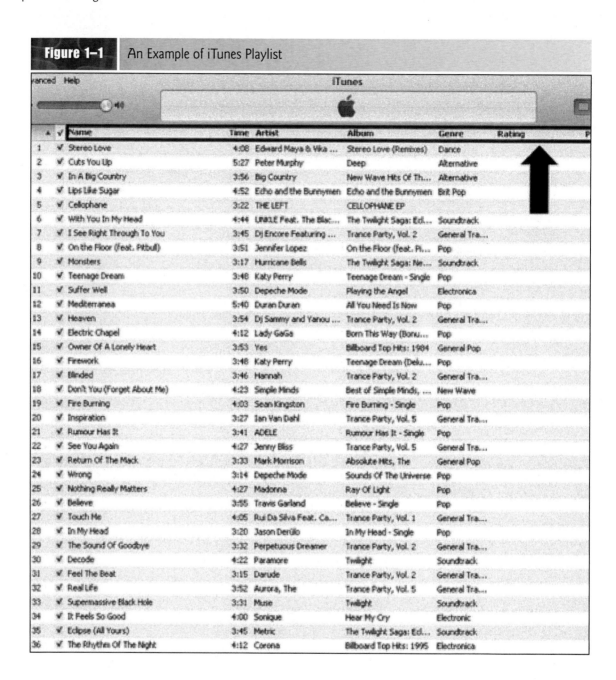

Figure 1–1   An Example of iTunes Playlist

familiar with the organization systems used by college course catalogs, grocery stores, iTunes, and libraries. Consider iTunes for example: iTunes allows you to organize your music into various playlists. Figure 1–1 illustrates the ways iTunes allows you to further organize your music within a playlist.

WHAT ARE SOME WAYS TO ORGANIZE INFORMATION?

Information is often organized by using several criteria. One basic question can be asked about many information systems: is the information in the system arranged by **content** or by physical **format?**

Content is the most common approach to arranging information. When you want more than one piece of information about a subject, you have to have some way of finding many items grouped together because they all have the same content. An example of organization by content, outside a library, is a college course catalog that allows you to find courses by subject, major, or requirements.

Format refers to the medium used to present or store information. Information comes in many configurations: it is audible (you heard it on the radio), visual (you are reading this text), and audio-visual (you watched it on YouTube).

Each of these configurations is stored as a physical format, and within each there are variations like mp3 or CD, microfilm or paper, and color or black-and-white. Resources found on the Web provide information in yet another format. Formats affect the ease of access to information and can be used as another way to organize it. A brief discussion of organization by physical format can be found near the end of this chapter.

Content and Organization of Information

Content is:

1. the *subject* of the information in an item
2. the aspect of information which is
    a. factual or analytical
    b. subjective or objective
    c. primary or secondary

Most information systems use content, that is, subject, as the first criterion for their organization of materials. Examples of this include amazon.com, with clothing in one section and electronics in another; and libraries, with books arranged by subject.

Many businesses use subject-based organization systems for storage because it simplifies **access** to their goods. Information systems are no different. You often seek information by subject:

- What's the phone number of a pizza delivery service? You look up "pizza" online.
- What movies are playing in town? You look on the pages of the local newspaper that advertise entertainment or go to the local theater's Web site.

In libraries materials are grouped by subject because it simplifies your search for more than one item about your topic. Once you learn how a particular system arranges its subjects you are able to search efficiently for your information needs, from pizza delivery to articles for a research paper assignment.

There are variations among subject-based organization systems. A good way to learn about a new system is to compare it to one you already know.

CONCEPT CHECK:

The value of organization is to make things easier to retrieve. Think of your playlist. If it's organized, you know how nice that is. If not, you know how hard it is to find a specific song.

LIBRARY CLASSIFICATION SYSTEMS

The Dewey Decimal System

One subject-based information system with which many people are familiar is the Dewey Decimal Classification System. This system organizes information by looking at the subject content of books and assigning numbers to those subjects. These numbers, call numbers, represent the location of a book in the library. Schools and public libraries often use this system to organize their books. You know how to use this system: you get the call number for a book, you search for that number in the stacks, or on the rows of bookshelves and retrieve the book. That is how any library's subject-based information system works.

The Library of Congress (LC) Classification System

The subject-based system used in most college and university libraries and in some large public libraries is the Library of Congress Classification System, or "LC" system. LC differs from the Dewey Decimal System in that it uses letters *and* numbers in its call numbers. LC's alphanumeric system results in the capability to expand far beyond a system that uses only numbers. Figure 1–2 shows several classification systems.

When you discover the call number range for a particular subject, all the materials that share that call number range are about the same subject. An online catalog can make this fact work for you before you go to the stacks. Once you have the call number of one book on your topic, see if you can search in the catalog by call number, and search under the first line of the call number; e.g., HD7102.U4. When you do such a search you get a list of all the titles that share that first line and therefore share the subject. You have just virtually browsed in the stacks, an activity that allows you to learn how much the library has on your subject, without ever going to the library. Of course, you can also browse by actually going to the library's bookshelves and looking at the books near the one with the call number you have.

Browsing helps you discover if the first book with the call number you found is really the best for your information need. Figure 1–4 shows the letters that begin the call numbers for materials on various subjects. You can use these letters to find the general area that contains resources on your topic.

| **FIGURE 1-2** | Common Classification Systems: LC, Dewey Decimal, NLM, and SuDocs |

Classification System	Library of Congress (LC)	Dewey Decimal	National Library of Medicine	Superintendent of Documents
Call Number	HD7102.U4 C5834 1982	368.382 PIL	W 100 F712i 2002	HE 22.26/3:13
Title	Compulsory health insurance: the continuing American debate	The new health insurance solution: how to get cheaper, better coverage without a traditional employer plan	Insurance handbook for the medical office	Health services utilization in the U.S. population by health insurance coverage

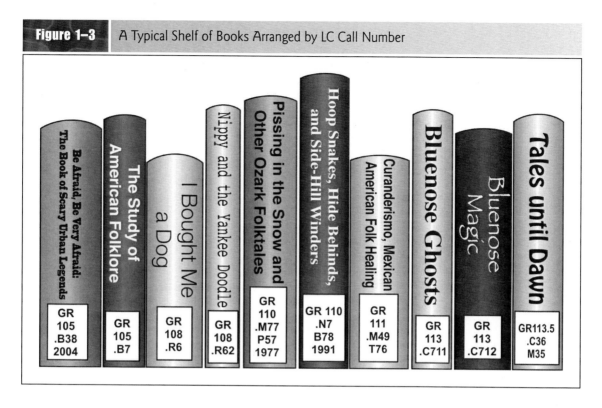

Figure 1-3 A Typical Shelf of Books Arranged by LC Call Number

The U.S. Superintendent of Documents (SuDocs) Classification System

Many college libraries include publications from the federal government in their holdings. The United States government is the world's largest publisher of information and libraries provide public access to these vast holdings. These publications are often shelved in a separate section of the library using another classification system that is almost, but not quite, a subject-based system. It is the U.S. Superintendent of Documents (SuDocs) Classification System. SuDocs numbers perform the same task that LC call numbers do: they group publications together on the shelves, but they do it by Cabinet-level agency rather than by subject.

Many libraries include the bibliographic records of their government publications in their catalogs. Now that you know about their unique numbering system, when you learn their location in your library you will realize that you have discovered a very rich source for information.

National Library of Medicine (NLM) Classification System

Many hospital and health sciences libraries use the NLM classification system to organize their materials. "The NLM Classification is a system of mixed notation patterned after the Library of Congress (LC) Classification where alphabetical letters which denote broad subject categories are further subdivided by numbers." http://www.nlm.nih.gov/pubs/factsheet/nlmclassif.html

SKILL CHECK:

Go to the S (Agriculture) call number range in your library and browse the stacks. Write down the complete call number and title of one book.

Figure 1–4	Subject Fields by Discipline, with Library of Congress Classification Letters

Sciences

General Q

Agriculture	S	Environmental Science	TD-TJ
Astronomy	QB	Food and Nutrition	TX
Biology	QH-QR	Geology	QE
Biochemistry	QH, QD, QP	Hearing and Speech	QP, RC, RF
Biophysics	QH	Mathematics	QA
Microbiology	QR	Medicine	R
Chemistry	QD	Medical Technology	RB
Computer Science	QA76, TK	Nursing	RT
Ecology	QH	Physics	QC
Engineering	TA-TN		

Social sciences

General H

Anthropology	GF-GT	Geography	G-GF
Business	HF-HJ	Law	K
Accounting	HF	Political Science	J-JX
Finance	HG	Psychology	BF, RC
Hotel & Restaurant Management	TX	Behavioral	BF
Management	HD	Clinical	RC
Marketing	HF	Sociology	HM-HX
Canadian Studies	F	Child-Family Studies	HQ
Economics	HB-HC	Criminology/Criminal Justice	HV
Education	L-LJ	Human Services	HV
Counseling	LB, BF	Social Work	HV
Elementary Education	LB	Sports	GV
Secondary Education	LB	Women's Studies	HQ
Special Education	LC		
Health Education	LB		

Humanities

(No General Area for ALL Humanities)

Art	N	English Literature	PR
Graphic Arts	NC	French Language	PQ
Photography	TR	French Literature	PQ
Communications/Mass Media	P, PN	German Language	PF
History	C-F	German Literature	PT
Latin America, Canada	F	Spanish Language	PC
Non-American	D	Spanish Literature	PQ
United States	E, F	Music	M
Literature/Languages	P-PT	Philosophy	B-BD, BH-BJ
American Literature	PS	Religion	BL-BX
English Literature	PE	Theater	PN

Miscellaneous

Biographies	CT	Library Science	Z
Bibliographies	Z	Military & Naval Sciences	U-V
Encyclopedias	AE		

HOW IS THE WEB ORGANIZED?

There is no one system that organizes the information on the Web. There are billions of Web pages housed on servers all over the world and accessible—with some limits—to people all over the world. Webpage makers create their pages and put them on a server. Some Internet Service Providers (ISPs) include providing a server to host webpages as one of the services to their subscribers; other web-pages are hosted on the servers of corporations or educational institutions. You can easily see how the number of pages on the Web continues to multiply. There is no requirement of most webpage makers that they provide any words that searchers could use to discover their pages. Finding the pages is a job most users leave to the search engines that can search the Web.

There are organization systems in place on many websites. If you go to the main page for a college, for example, you'll find an organization system in place on that site, usually aimed at prospective and current students and therefore organized according to how students are most likely to seek and use the college's information.

But is the Web as a whole organized? No. It is not.

The LC system, and to a lesser extent, the SuDocs system, rely on content to arrange infor-mation materials by subject. Using characteristics of the content to more finely arrange information resources can make your research easier.

Research projects are common college assignments. A research assignment is meant to give you an opportunity to demonstrate to your professor that you are able to locate information re-sources about the course's topics and to synthesize information from different resources. The final product, the research paper or report, allows you to present your understanding of the resources and the topic, showing the professor that you have grown intellectually from the course. This chapter will provide guidelines for selecting materials that you will then be able to synthesize as part of your research project, and you need to know that research is an iterative process.

THE RESEARCH PROCESS

The *Merriam-Webster Online Dictionary* defines process as "a series of actions or operations con-ducing to an end."

Research is, indeed, a process; thus, the information research process is the series of steps you perform to retrieve relevant information. If you are aware of the process of research you will be bet-ter able to make the steps work to your advantage.

The **basic steps of information research** are these:

- Identify your research topic
- Determine the information requirements for your assignment
- Locate and retrieve relevant information resources
- Evaluate information resources
- Cite your sources

 SEARCH TIP

Google uses a proprietary algorithm to determine websites' page rank in your results. This algo-rithm is based on how long the page has existed, the number of pages that link to it, and the number of keywords matching your search terms.

You go through these steps every time you do research whether or not you are aware of it. Even when you use *Yahoo!* and retrieve only webpages for an assignment, you have run through the process in your mind. In order to do top-notch research, however, you might want to look at the steps more carefully.

Examining the Process

Identify Your Research Topic

What are you looking for? What are the concepts you are researching? You will use the topic/subject/discipline relationship in this step to examine the concepts you discover in your topic.

Determine the Information Requirements for Your Assignment

Every researcher has the awareness and common sense that help determine the information requirements for all assignments.

This step compels you to pay attention to both your topic and your assignment. It requires you to be aware of your intended audience; i.e., those who will read your paper or listen to your presentation. Is the course for which you are doing the assignment a first-year introductory one such as SOC 101, or an advanced seminar such as HIS 464? How technical or advanced is the reader of the paper or the members of the audience for your speech? If you are researching a topic for personal use, with whom will you share what you learn? Is the audience as knowledgeable as you are about the topic or do you—and they—need introductory information? You must look at these parameters and also use common sense to determine what type of information you need.

MAKING YOUR TOPIC WORK

You do information research every day and many times each day. For instance, every time you search *Facebook,* you are doing research. But what about **scholarly research?** There are several components to scholarly research.

- First you must refine your topic to make it workable with the information tools you will use while staying within the guidelines of your research assignment (e.g., your professor said you have to use "scholarly sources").
- You must devise a search strategy. This means that you will have to make a series of decisions about where and how to look for information on your topic.
- You must select appropriate information tools. You have to figure out which tools have the best information about your particular topic; there probably will be more than one that can give you what you are looking for. Your topic must be your guide in selecting the tools that you use.

Because the topic is a fundamental factor in some research decisions, you need to examine it closely.

ASPECTS OF A TOPIC, CONTEXTS FOR A TOPIC

Focusing on a single aspect of a topic results in a paper that will be easier to write because all the information you gather will have that same focus.

What angle or aspect of the topic do you want to examine? Very often a topic does not seem broad until you start to research it, at which point you discover that almost all topics have many aspects that can be researched and you are going to have to choose only one. Your decision about your angle on the topic is a crucial one. Even topics that seem more focused than obviously broad ones have aspects which, when you choose one, can narrow your focus and make your research more manageable.

Often you need to put your topic into a broader context before you can break it apart into manageable aspects. This may sound contradictory, but it is not. Knowing the academic discipline or broader context into which your topic fits helps you select the search tools that will be most helpful. It also rescues a too-narrow topic by showing you where to look for help to broaden it.

One way for you to figure out the subject field of any topic is to determine which college department might teach a course on it. This will not always be the same department as the one whose course gave you the assignment. College departments correspond to subject fields in many information systems and the fields are related in turn to search tools and resources. Figure 1–5 shows some aspects of a very broad topic, drugs, with the college departments/subject fields that may be related to each aspect.

Relating your topic to a subject field is not always easy, but once you learn how to discover such a relationship, you can move more quickly to the tools and resources that are particular to your topic's field. For example, for the drugs topic you would know to look for information about educating patients about drugs in nursing resources rather than looking for a book on prescription drugs.

GETTING HELP IN ANALYZING YOUR TOPIC: TOOLS FOR RESEARCH

Encyclopedias and the introductory sections in books can provide a context for a topic, as well as an overview of its major aspects.

How can you find out what aspects there are to a topic? You can use an **encyclopedia** that gives you an objective overview of the whole subject field for your topic. One point to remember is that most topics do not have their own encyclopedias. Information about a topic can be found in an encyclopedia that covers the topic's subject field. For example, you would not find a complete encyclopedia on the Kentucky rifle, but you would find information about that particular rifle in an encyclopedia on weaponry. Your topic is the rifle and the subject field is weaponry. A topic will be included in an encyclopedia that covers your subject field, although there might not be a whole encyclopedia about every topic.

Another information resource in this category that can serve as a research tool is the introductory section in a general book on your subject field. It too can provide a broad overview of the topics in the field.

If you are unable to find specifics on your original topic in its subject field, or if what you find is too specific, what alternatives do you have? You can go to the discipline in which your subject field fits and look for information there. In information research the word discipline refers to one of

CONCEPT CHECK

Consider who will hear your presentation or read your paper. This can influence your search choices.

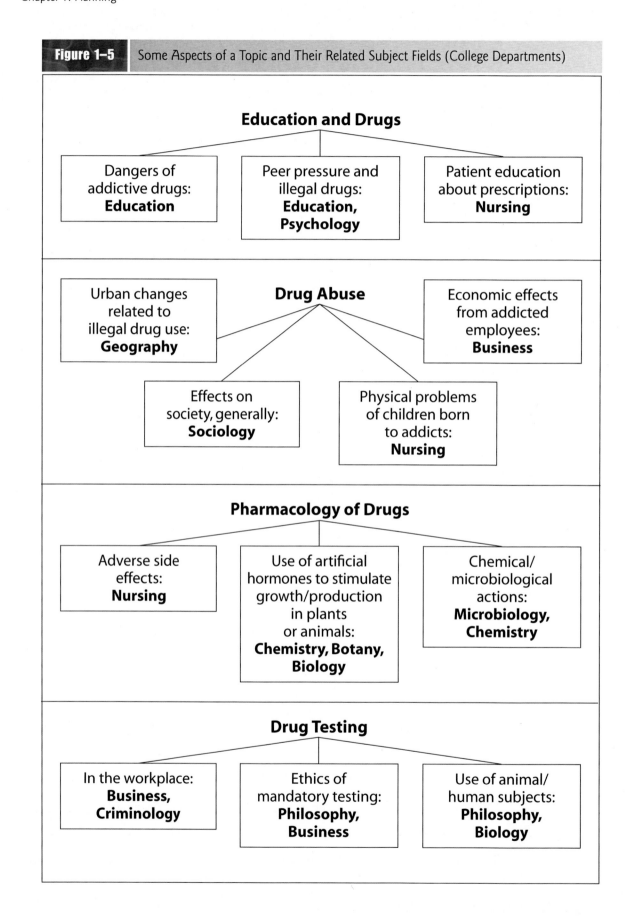

Figure 1–5 Some Aspects of a Topic and Their Related Subject Fields (College Departments)

three major divisions of knowledge. **The disciplines are the Sciences, the Social Sciences, and the Humanities.**

The Sciences discipline includes the hard science subject fields, such as physics, computer science, and medicine. Soft sciences, such as demographics and political science, are parts of the Social Sciences discipline. The Humanities include all the arts—visual, literary, and performing, and other subject fields such as religion and philosophy. It is pretty easy to put some subject fields into their appropriate disciplines: mathematics and biology are parts of the Sciences; sociology and education fit into the Social Sciences; literature, theater, and languages, including English, are considered part of Humanities.

There are other subject fields that fit into more than one discipline. One such **interdisciplinary** subject field is anthropology. Anthropology deals with social and cultural studies (Social Sciences) and with archaeology which may be considered part of history (Humanities). The subject field of Women's Studies, in turn, can be included in either the Social Sciences or Humanities.

Look again at Figure 1–4. This chart also presents commonly accepted subject field/discipline relationships. In each of the three disciplines there is an abbreviated list of its subject fields and the letters that represent the subject fields' Library of Congress classifications—the letters that begin their LC call number(s).

The Kentucky rifle topic mentioned earlier is part of the subject field of weaponry. This interdisciplinary subject field could fall into the Sciences—the technology of ordnance—or the Humanities—the history of weaponry. You can see how knowing the relationship of your topic to its subject field and discipline provides flexibility for you to focus your search on a selected area.

An example of the subject field/discipline relationship is encountered on the websites of many college libraries. They list the databases to which they subscribe by subject and discipline. Figure 1–6 shows one college library's subject list of journal databases. When you click on a subject, the list of databases by subject field within that discipline opens, as shown by the inset in Figure 1–6.

INFORMATION CHARACTERISTICS AND YOUR INFORMATION NEED

One of the first steps you take in your information research is defining your information need. You figure out what you need, usually just in your head and not yet on paper. Consider the aspects of information that were mentioned earlier. Do you need **analytical** information or **factual** information,

SEARCH TIP

Knowing the relationship of your topic to its subject field and discipline enables you to choose a search tool appropriate to your topic.

SKILL CHECK

Which discipline includes your major?

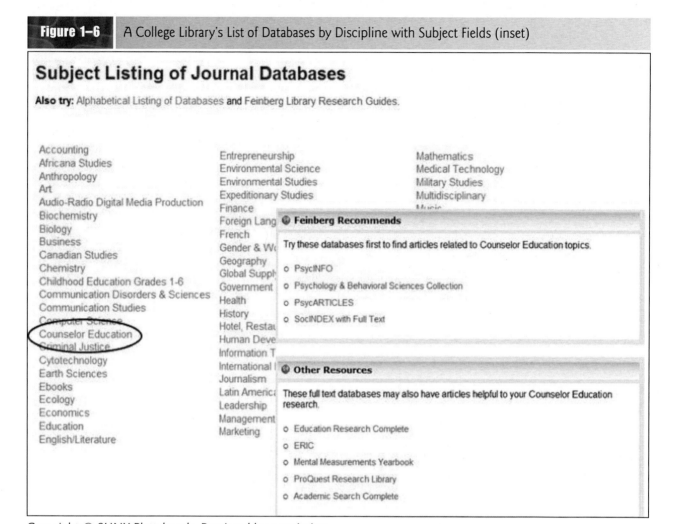

Figure 1–6   A College Library's List of Databases by Discipline with Subject Fields (inset)

Copyright © SUNY Plattsburgh. Reprinted by permission.

subjective information or **objective, primary** or **secondary** information? You may never have asked yourself these questions in exactly these words, but you are aware of these distinctions and how the answers to them affect your information research. If you are aware of what type of information you need, and some of its characteristics, you will make good decisions right from the beginning of your research.

Factual or Analytical

Factual information is made up of facts, and a fact is "something known to exist or to have happened," according to the *American Heritage Dictionary*. Factual information can provide answers to questions such as, "Who won the Pulitzer Prize for Fiction in 2013?" or "What are the main characters' names in the novel *Twilight?*" A purely factual information source provides no explanation of its statements. The federal government produces many publications that fall into this category, as do numerous other publishers.

When you decide that you need only factual information you are likely to seek short-answer resources. These resources include dictionaries, atlases, handbooks, and directories, and will usually be found in a library's reference room or reference collection. The reference collection can be both a print collection and online sources. Many college libraries have clearly labeled reference collections. The collections may include titles such as the CIA's *World Factbook, Merriam-Webster Online (dictionary),* and the *Occupational Outlook Handbook.*

Reference resources are often kept separate from the other books in a library and clearly labeled on many library websites because their content makes them most useful in a quick-look-up way. For example, you would not read the *Dictionary of Concepts in General Psychology* from cover to cover to discover Freud's place in psychology. Rather you use the book briefly in the reference area of the library to get that information. Nor should you have to check out a book such as *International Marketing Data and Statistics* for four weeks when you can open it to one page and see the table that lists the number of cinema screens and cinema revenue per country. This book is shelved in a reference area or its link may be in an online version of a reference collection. The online reference collection does not duplicate the material in the reference area—the print and online collections are distinct.

Some reference sources include factual information that has been put into a broader context. Encyclopedias and some handbooks comprise this type of resource and provide **background information.** They give you overviews of topics. Encyclopedias, by presenting the various aspects of a topic and the known viewpoints in a subject field, can help you focus your research on the one aspect of your original topic that most interests you. Not only do encyclopedias provide the various facets of a subject field but most often they also use the terminology that is common to the field. Those terms can provide you with new ways to find materials on your topic.

Analytical information is an interpretation of facts. Your professor provides an analysis when she explains the meaning of a paragraph in your philosophy text. Analytical information includes interpretations of facts, usually by experts, such as the discussions you find on blogs and in periodical articles and books examining the implications of, for example, the Arab Spring. Analytical information is found in books and periodical articles, and on blogs written by experts and others in various fields.

A search for analytical information requires information from periodical articles and books and blogs and perhaps government publications that discuss the interrelations among, implications of, and reasons behind actions, ideas, works of art, and events. Usually it takes more than one resource to provide a thorough analysis of a topic, so you as a researcher will have to find a system that groups items of the same subject together. Your familiarity with organization systems will help you find resources grouped together on a topic.

 SEARCH TIP

Background sources, such as Wikipedia or other encyclopedias, provide factual information within a context, and are excellent places to begin research on a topic that's new to you.

SKILL CHECK

Identify three encyclopedias—other than general ones such as Wikipedia or Encyclopedia Britannica—available to you.

Objective or Subjective

Another characteristic of information is its subjectivity or objectivity. Opinions or personal viewpoints comprise **subjective** information, while non-judgmental and balanced reporting is considered **objective** information. An example of the difference between subjective and objective information sources might be your friend's opinion on illegal immigration (subjective source) and statistics found in the *Encyclopedia of American Immigration* (objective source). When do you need one and when should you seek the other?

Objective information often enables you to choose a single aspect of a topic that will be manageable for your research because it should present all sides of a topic. Objective information usually includes basic facts within a clear context that provides you with a sense of the whole topic. Many encyclopedias strive to provide just this type of objective help.

Subjective information often presents limited perspectives on a topic. An editorial, for instance, provides subjective information; it gives the writer's opinion. A review of several subjective sources enables you to understand a range of opinions on a topic and helps you to determine bias in an argument. These opinions might include:

- A Yelp or Trip Advisor review
- A book review in Amazon
- A scientist's comments about a colleague's research findings
- An editorial in a newspaper or journal

Subjective information often provides assistance when your job is to evaluate a subject. Most subjective information is found in (non-reference) books and periodical articles. Many Web sites provide subjective information. For example, a site found at *www.globalwarming.org* is sponsored by the Cooler Heads Coalition, a sub-group of the National Consumer Coalition. Such a group will provide information on its Web site that supports *its* (subjective) view of the topic.

You already know the difference between objective or subjective, and analytical or factual information. You demonstrate this knowledge by asking a friend for his review of the local pizza places (subjective) and not taking out a book on pizza (objective), and by looking online or in the reference collection of a library when you need only a definition or a statistic (factual), rather than checking out books or reading blogs (analytical).

Primary or Secondary

Sometimes you are assigned to find and analyze raw data in a research project, or to locate and use the first report of a scientific breakthrough. Other times you have a personal wish to see an on-the-scene account of an incident. These are instances of needs for primary information sources. What is primary information and how does it differ from secondary? How does this affect its place in an information system, and therefore affect your information research?

CONCEPT CHECK

Consider some sources of information you might find on immigration, such as a blog, textbook, and a ship's passenger list. Are these subjective or objective sources of information?

Primary information is information in its original form. A primary source provides information that has not been published anywhere else, or put into a context, or interpreted, or translated by anyone else. Examples of primary sources are:

- People, such as the professor who tells you about what happened in the class you missed because you were ill
- Accounts of events written by reporters on the scene, such as the Web site and newspaper articles about the Iditarod sled-dog race in Alaska
- A first report of a scientific study, such as the medical journal article that first reported the research that discovered the causative virus in AIDS
- An original artwork or photograph
- A handwritten letter, such as the example in Figure 1–7a
- A diary, Twitter stream, or blog, as illustrated in Figure 1-7b (A diary might be considered an old-fashioned non-electronic version of a blog.)

Primary information is a first appearance of information and much of its value as a source derives from this fact. Some primary sources are original manuscripts and letters that require special preservation techniques. These sources are very often fragile or rare and may be kept in a library's Special Collections or Archives, or in a library that is itself a special collection. Many of these fragile resources are now appearing on the Web, digitized so that they can be used by many and yet not be damaged by handling. While the digitized image itself is a reprocessing of the original, you, as an undergraduate student, might be allowed to cite it as a primary source if your professor knows the format in which you used it.

Figure 1–7a Letter from Abraham Lincoln to Mary Todd Lincoln

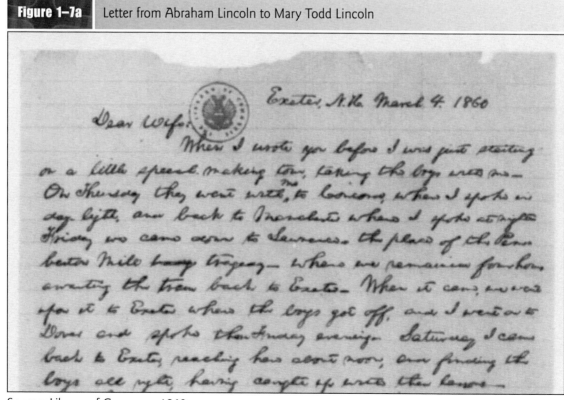

Source: Library of Congress, 1860

| **Figure 1–7b** | Primary Source: SUNY Plattsburgh EHHS Dean's Blog |

From http://ehhsdean.wordpress.com by Dr. Michael Morgan. Copyright © 2012 by Dr. Michael Morgan. Reprinted by permission.

Secondary information is a restatement, examination, or interpretation of information from one or more primary sources. It has been removed in some way from its original (primary) source and repackaged. Examples of secondary sources include:

- A friend who provides her notes to you from the class you missed (she interpreted what the professor said and passed that interpretation on to you)
- A documentary that follows the Iditarod and explores how it is won relatively often by women mushers
- A newspaper article that summarizes a journal article on the AIDS virus
- A student's research paper that uses reviews to critique a painting or novel
- A journal article discussing the literary merit of diaries and blogs

Secondary sources also include information tools that lead you to primary information, such as periodical indexes or bibliographies that cite primary works. For example, a bibliography of diaries is a secondary source because it is a list of diaries, not the diaries themselves, and it provides you with enough information to allow you to find the primary sources, the diaries. Anyone who does genealogical research is familiar with indexes that help find particular issues of old newspapers with information about their family histories; those indexes are secondary sources. Books and blogs are often considered secondary sources because they analyze and synthesize information taken from other sources. See Figure 1–8. Be aware that books and other sources also may be considered primary sources because they are the first publication of a particular synthesis.

Here are some definitions of primary and secondary information from the information experts at the American Library Association. Primary sources are "original records created at the time historical events occurred or well after events in the form of memoirs and oral histories . . . and may include letters, manuscripts, diaries, journals, newspapers, speeches, interviews, memoirs, documents produced by government agencies such as Congress or the Office of the President, photo-

Figure 1–8 Secondary Source: An Analytical Blog

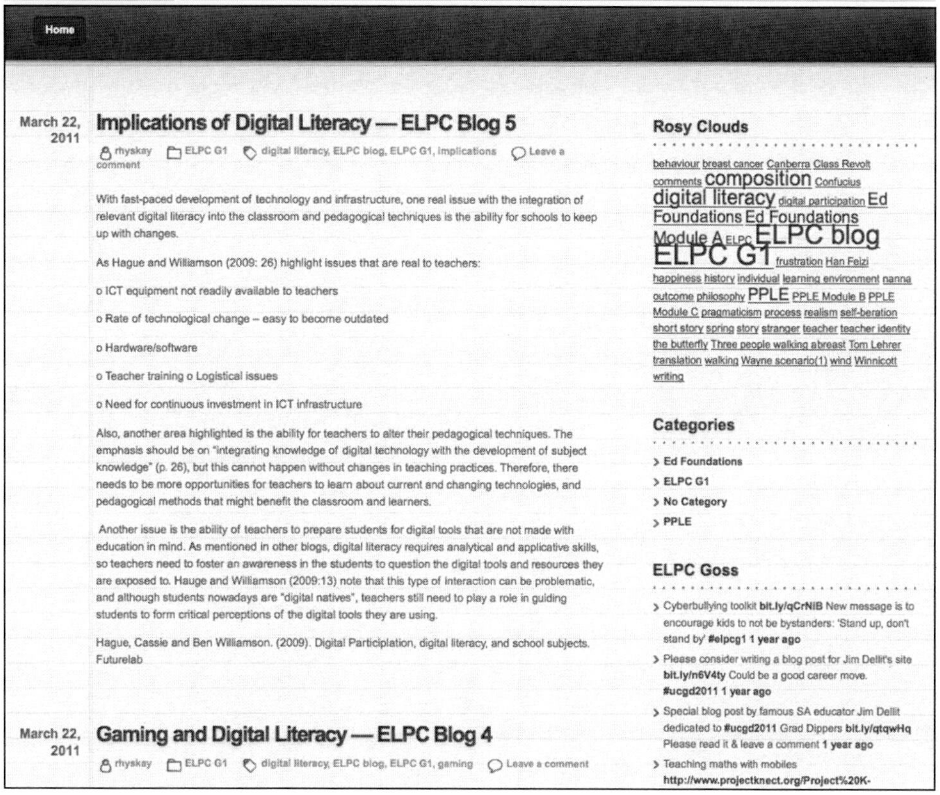
Home

March 22, 2011

Implications of Digital Literacy — ELPC Blog 5

rhyskay ELPC G1 digital literacy, ELPC blog, ELPC G1, implications Leave a comment

With fast-paced development of technology and infrastructure, one real issue with the integration of relevant digital literacy into the classroom and pedagogical techniques is the ability for schools to keep up with changes.

As Hague and Williamson (2009: 26) highlight issues that are real to teachers:

o ICT equipment not readily available to teachers

o Rate of technological change – easy to become outdated

o Hardware/software

o Teacher training o Logistical issues

o Need for continuous investment in ICT infrastructure

Also, another area highlighted is the ability for teachers to alter their pedagogical techniques. The emphasis should be on "integrating knowledge of digital technology with the development of subject knowledge" (p. 26), but this cannot happen without changes in teaching practices. Therefore, there needs to be more opportunities for teachers to learn about current and changing technologies, and pedagogical methods that might benefit the classroom and learners.

Another issue is the ability of teachers to prepare students for digital tools that are not made with education in mind. As mentioned in other blogs, digital literacy requires analytical and applicative skills, so teachers need to foster an awareness in the students to question the digital tools and resources they are exposed to. Hauge and Williamson (2009:13) note that this type of interaction can be problematic, and although students nowadays are "digital natives", teachers still need to play a role in guiding students to form critical perceptions of the digital tools they are using.

Hague, Cassie and Ben Williamson. (2009). Digital Participlation, digital literacy, and school subjects. Futurelab

March 22, 2011

Gaming and Digital Literacy — ELPC Blog 4

rhyskay ELPC G1 digital literacy, ELPC blog, ELPC G1, gaming Leave a comment

Rosy Clouds

behaviour breast cancer Canberra Class Revolt comments composition Confucius digital literacy digital participation Ed Foundations Ed Foundations Module A ELPC ELPC blog ELPC G1 frustration Han Feizi happiness history individual learning environment nanna outcome philosophy PPLE PPLE Module B PPLE Module C pragmatism process realism self-beration short story spring story stranger teacher teacher identity the butterfly Three people walking abreast Tom Lehrer translation walking Wayne scenario(1) wind Winnicott writing

Categories

› Ed Foundations
› ELPC G1
› No Category
› PPLE

ELPC Goss

› Cyberbullying toolkit bit.ly/qCrNiB New message is to encourage kids to not be bystanders: 'Stand up, don't stand by' #elpcg1 1 year ago
› Please consider writing a blog post for Jim Dellit's site bit.ly/n6V4ty Could be a good career move. #ucgd2011 1 year ago
› Special blog post by famous SA educator Jim Dellit dedicated to #ucgd2011 Grad Dippers bit.ly/qtqwHq Please read it & leave a comment 1 year ago
› Teaching maths with mobiles http://www.projectknect.org/Project%20K-

http://scholarsdenwenlin.wordpress.com/

graphs, audio recordings, moving pictures or video recordings, research data, and objects or artifacts such as works of art or ancient roads, buildings, tools, and weapons." Primary sources are often important in fields such as history, where contemporary accounts of events and ideas may differ from present-day accounts of those same events and ideas, and in science, where primary reports provide research that is then built upon by later research. Secondary sources are "any material other than primary sources used in the preparation of a written work" (Young, 1983, p. 176, 201). Raw data such as statistics that have been collected but not analyzed, first reports of research studies, original artworks, online news reports, newspaper, magazine, and journal accounts of a subject comprise primary information and are frequently found by using secondary sources.

Because the definition of primary source can differ from subject to subject; e.g., from History to Biology, be sure to ask your professor for a definition of the term when you are required to use a primary source for your research assignment.

PHYSICAL FORMAT AND ORGANIZATION OF INFORMATION

One common way to organize information resources is by **format.** The basic concept behind a format-based information system is this: the physical attributes of items determine where they go. For example, you do not store your video recordings on your heater or on your drafty windowsill; the formats of the recordings helped you make the organizational decision to keep them in a place with a more stable temperature.

PLANNING AND SELECTING THE RIGHT TYPES OF INFORMATION

Books

Books generally provide in-depth and lengthy coverage on a given subject. Because of the amount of time involved to write and publish, the information is not always up-to-the-minute. This is only a concern if you are researching a topic that requires the most current information available. If you are unsure of the merit of a book, consult a book review published in a professional journal of the given subject area.

Newspapers

Daily newspapers are a great source for information on current events, such as the European Debt Crisis. Older editions provide day-to-day coverage of past events such as the terrorist attacks on America on September 11, 2001 and the BP oil spill in the Gulf of Mexico in 2010. Because newspapers are outlets of mass communication, they're good barometers for reading the interests of the popular culture.

Periodicals

Like newspapers, periodicals are good sources for current information because they are published frequently. Periodicals differ from newspapers in that many periodicals are professional journals devoted to a specific field of study, such as *Journal of Protozoology*. Articles appearing in these journals are much more authoritative than comparative newspaper articles as most have very stringent review processes for submission. Compared to books, periodical articles tend to focus on a specific aspect of a topic, and are less useful for general overviews or histories of a topic.

Web Sources

The Web is a great resource for getting current information on a variety of topics because it links to so many different content providers and be sure to check when the site was last updated. A commercial domain (.com) may be less reliable than an educational (.edu) or government (.gov) domain. If the site on a current issue was last updated several months ago, chances are the information contained within the site has been superseded. The Web is useful for finding information on associations and companies, but remember to pay attention to who has authored the web page.

U.S. Government Publications

U.S. government publications are excellent sources of information on a variety of topics, such as business, science, law, criminal justice, etc. Many primary documents, published under the auspices of the federal government, provide vital information such as census data, Supreme Court transactions, and federal rules and regulations. Policy statements and resources are often listed on agency web sites for citizen use as well.

Dissertations

Dissertations generally cover a narrow topic but do so in great detail. The authority of the work is generally without question as all are produced under the guidance of an academic committee within a university. To gauge the value of the information to a given field of study, check to see if it was later published as a scholarly book. A published dissertation has made it through the extra review process of a particular press, and therefore, it is likely to be more authoritative than a similar paper that has not been published.

Revised from **Planning and Selecting the Right Types of Information** by Holly Heller-Ross, Feinberg Library, Plattsburgh State, 2008. Adapted with permission from a guide written by David Seiller at the University at Albany 7/98. <http://www.plattsburgh.edu/files/451/files/Resources.pdf>

Format here refers to the physical form of an information source. Major formats are:

- Books, mainly bound volumes
- Periodicals subdivided into:
  - Unbound loose issues
  - Microformats (microfilm or microfiche)
  - Bound paper volumes
- Media, including many technologies used in information storage and retrieval, such as CDs and DVDs
- Online resources, including e-books, encyclopedias, and e-journals

Periodicals, Media, and Government Publications

In many places, not just libraries, periodicals, journals, or serials are kept separate from books. A **periodical, journal,** or **serial** is an information resource that is published periodically; i.e., on a regular (daily, weekly, monthly, quarterly) basis. A bookstore uses racks to display the magazines it sells and often keeps them near a cashier's station, while it keeps its books on shelves throughout the store. In your home you may handle the magazines you buy or subscribe to differently from the way you handle your books. In the same way, libraries often have a periodicals collection that consists of magazines, journals, and newspapers, and that is separate from the book stacks. Periodicals are frequently in microformats that may or may not be located near the paper periodicals. Microfilm and microfiche make up the microformats that are used commonly to preserve older volumes of some periodicals.

Media materials comprise another category that is handled differently from books and periodicals. Libraries may have separate sections where media is shelved.

Government Publications are frequently separated from a library's main book collection because of the way the issuing government (International, Federal, State, or Local) dictates that they must be handled by the library. Libraries that accept free U.S. Government publications must make them accessible to the public and those collections are usually shelved separately using the SuDocs classification system.

FINDING INFORMATION SOURCES IN DIFFERENT ORGANIZATION SYSTEMS

At any of the libraries you use, you need to know which organization systems are used in order to find the material you want. This means that you must know if:

- Your library uses Dewey Decimal or LC call numbers in its main book collection
- Your library keeps its periodicals in an area separate from the main book collection
- The periodicals are organized alphabetically or by call number
- Media such as sound- and video-recordings are shelved with books or in a different location
- Government publications are given LC call numbers and are shelved with books, or if they follow the publications' unique numbering systems and are shelved in their own space
- There are smaller areas that repeat the major system, such as the reference area and special collections that use LC call numbers

 SEARCH TIP

Before you search, consider the characteristics of the information you need. This will make your research more efficient.

A tour, whether a formal guided tour, an online tour, or an informal walk around your library, is one of the best approaches to learning how things are organized and where they are in your library. To get the most from your tour, consider the following:

- Can you find a book in the stacks after you have learned how to get its call number from the library's catalog?
- If you need a quick fact, are there resources in the reference area? Does the reference collection use LC call numbers?
- Where can you use the databases and other indexes that will help you find information on your topic?
- How can you tell if the library has the latest issue of a periodical you need or subscribes to an online journal you want?
- Can you check out DVDs from the library? And are there any popular movies available?
- What other services does the library offer that you can use—photocopying, interlibrary loans, scanning, wireless Internet access?

Be sure to locate the research or reference desk so that you know where to find librarians when you have questions!

Your understanding of the concepts that are used to organize information will contribute to your ease in doing information research. It will make your work in the library and with online information materials efficient and productive.

This chapter includes a lot of information that many researchers may see as complicated. You may be tempted to continue to go to the computer and type in your topic, accept the references from the first screen or two that appear, and go on your way. You may not run into trouble with this approach until you reach the end of your work—the writing of the paper or presentation. Then there is a good chance you will have to work hard to tie together the disparate ideas from the materials you have collected with no guarantee of success.

A good example of this situation is one in which a student needed to write a ten-page paper on poverty and use at least five resources. When they searched for information they typed poverty into a database and also into a search engine. They retrieved some articles from the database and a couple of interesting websites. As a result, they had to somehow connect 1) the article on single mothers and poverty to 2) the website from the Southern Poverty Law Center to 3) the article on homelessness to 4) the article on the connection between low income and drug use to 5) the website about trends in teen pregnancy. That would be a tough job, especially in ten pages. It would have been far easier to use an encyclopedia, maybe the *Encyclopedia of Sociology,* to discover some of the aspects in the huge topic of poverty. At this point they may have decided to focus on the connection between poverty and drug use. They then could have chosen a general database and a subject-oriented database such as *Sociological Abstracts*. The search results would likely have all been related to the same single aspect: poverty and drug use.

Thinking about a topic at the beginning of your research takes time. But it will pay off at the end, when you discover that you have focused your research enough to collect materials that you can relate to each other . . . and use to write a good paper.

SKILL CHECK

Give yourself a tour of your library. What are some of the ways in which your library is organized?

CHAPTER HIGHLIGHTS

- Organization provides access to information; it creates relationships among the items organized, and between the parts and the whole.

- A major criterion for organizing information is its subject matter, as used by the Library of Congress (LC) Classification System in libraries.

- Dewey Decimal, SuDocs, and NLM are other classification systems commonly used in libraries.

- Topic analysis involves determining what subject field you are really investigating early in your research because often the topic is one aspect of a larger subject field.

- Research areas can be grouped into three major categories or *disciplines;* they are the Sciences, the Social Sciences, and the Humanities.

- Some topics are "interdisciplinary," meaning that they fit into more than one discipline at the same time.

- You can begin your research in a resource that provides an overview of a field, such as an encyclopedia devoted to one subject field or discipline.

- The content of information resources can be described by its characteristics: factual or analytical, subjective or objective, and primary or secondary.

- Primary information is information in its original form, and secondary information is a repackaging of primary information through examination, interpretation, or analysis. This distinction can be important.

- It is common to organize information by format, meaning the physical configuration of the information, such as a library grouping together books, separate from periodicals and media.

- Types of information such as newspapers, blogs, books, journals, and dissertations are valuable for different purposes.

CHAPTER 1

Questions

1. Describe an organization system that you have established and used in your own life. Name each criterion for arrangement and explain why you used it.

2. Is the information available on the World Wide Web organized? Explain your answer.

3. Your professor has assigned a research paper on the effect of colonialism on North American indigenous peoples. Locate and provide author, title, and format information for one primary and one secondary source on this topic.

Searching

LEARNING OBJECTIVES

- Investigate the scope, content, and organization of information retrieval systems
- Select appropriate tools (e.g., indexes, online databases) for research on a particular topic
- Identify keywords, synonyms, and related terms for the information needed
- Identify and uses search language and protocols (e.g., Boolean, adjacency) appropriate to the retrieval system
- Explain what controlled vocabulary is and why it is used
- Demonstrate an understanding of the concept of Boolean logic and constructs a search statement using Boolean operators

SEARCH TOOLS

A tool is something you use to help you accomplish a task. When you are conducting research, your task may be to find different types of information. Search tools can help you accomplish this task by leading you to the information your research requires. Search tools may provide the actual resource that you need or they may give you only enough information, such as a citation, to find that resource. Common search tools include catalogs, databases, search engines, and bibliographies.

A **catalog** is a collection of records describing the resources in a library's collections, many of which are books. The records in any catalog provide descriptions of the items, such as the title, author, subject, and location in the library's collections. Catalogs use very similar formats for their descriptions, so that it is likely you will be able to transfer your knowledge of one library catalog to other library catalogs as well. This means that you will be able to locate materials in any type of library, whether it is your local public library or your college library.

Databases provide access to the contents of resources by describing and organizing the contents. These databases most commonly provide access to periodical articles. Many databases provide access to an article's entire text, the article's citation information, and an abstract, which is a short summary of the article. These databases are referred to as full text databases. Other types of databases, however, do not provide the entire article. An index provides only the information needed to find an article, such as a bibliographic citation, while an abstract database provides a citation as well as an abstract. See Figure 2–1 for an example of the references found in a bibliographic database.

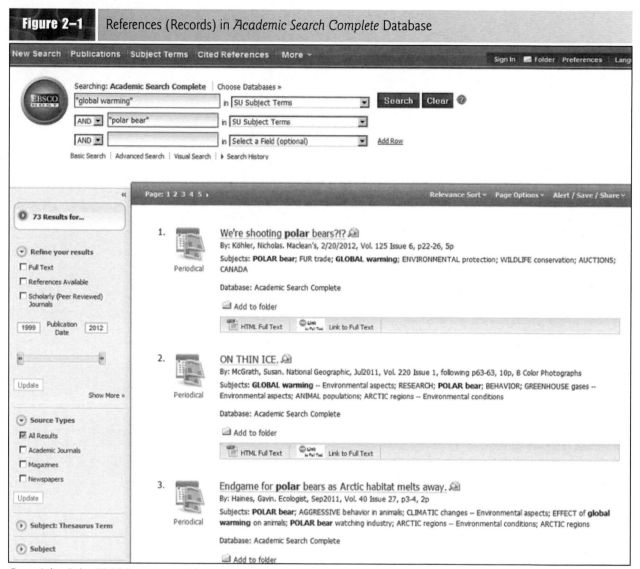

Figure 2–1   References (Records) in *Academic Search Complete* Database

Copyright © by EBSCO. Reprinted by permission.

THE SCOPE OF SEARCH TOOLS

One search tool may cover a wide range of topics or a narrow range of topics. The range of a search tool is called its **scope.** Tools with a broad scope have a little bit of information on everything; a more specific tool has more information on fewer things. For instance, a search tool can cover a single subject, a group of related subjects, or an entire discipline. Search tools that include many different subjects in a variety of disciplines are often referred to as multidisciplinary or general.

SKILL CHECK

Which citations in Figure 2–1 would link to full-text articles?

Depending on your topic, you might use subject-specific, discipline-specific, or general tools and resources, alone or in combination, in your information research. Other resources, such as encyclopedias and search engines, differ in scope as well. It is important that you select resources that have the scope most appropriate for your topic. For instance, a subject-specific database like *PsycInfo* may be the best choice for a student doing in-depth research for an evolutionary psychology class, whereas a broad-coverage database like *ProQuest Research Library* may be most helpful for a student researching a general topic like drunk driving for a public speaking class.

Search engines are among the most commonly used search tools. Three of the most popular search engines are *Google, Yahoo!* and *Bing.* It is important to remember that different search engines retrieve different results. Your results may be affected by your location, previous search history, and any privacy or security settings on your browser or network. A search engine like *Google* searches public websites for your search terms and returns all resources that include those terms. However, there are some important considerations to keep in mind when using search engines. Search engines often cannot retrieve resources located in the Invisible Web, such as faculty webpages or articles in library databases. Although you almost always find something on your topic by searching the Web, the percentage of relevant hits may be quite low, especially when hundreds of thousands of sites are found. There are numerous websites available that explain search engines and compare their work. A good explanation can be found in the *Wikipedia* <http://www.wikipedia.org> *but* you must remember that information on this website is subject to change. See also the *Search Engine Watch* site <http://www.searchenginewatch.com> for comparisons of various search engines.

One other search tool that is easily overlooked is a **bibliography,** of which there are several types. It can be the list of references found at the end of a book or at the end of a chapter in a book. A bibliography can also be found at the end of a periodical article or refer to the list of References you create at the end of your research paper. The type of bibliography at the end of an article can often be a useful search tool to find more information on your topic. A bibliography also can be a book-length list of materials on one subject (for example, *American Indian Studies, A Bibliographic Guide*), or materials by and about one author (for example, *J. R. R. Tolkien: A Descriptive Bibliography*). In those cases, a bibliography can do much of your work for you by providing you with a prepared list of resources on your topic. Bibliographies often allow you to locate older resources related to your topic; however, sometimes an item in your search results, such as an article or book chapter, may have a Cited By link. This link can be used to find other newer sources which have cited that particular source. It is useful to know how many times a source has been cited because it allows you to locate current research based on older research. It also allows you to determine the source's importance within that field of research; for example, a source that has been cited

CONCEPT CHECK

Identify one subject-specific database and one multidisciplinary database to which your library subscribes.

◆ **SEARCH TIP**

Always remember that no single search engine indexes the entire Web.

only once by other authors may be less prominent than a source that has been cited 200 times by other authors.

WHAT SEARCH TOOLS DO

Search tools provide access. In reality all of them index something. A search tool thus provides systematic access to the content of an information resource. You have often used an index in a book. Think of what you did. You looked under a person's name or an event or an idea in the Index in the back of the book. In this alphabetical list of names and subjects you found reference to the page(s) on which your person or event or idea was mentioned. You then went to the page(s) listed in the index because you knew there was information there on your person, event, or idea.

A single book's index is just a small index; it is a guide to the contents of that book only. A library's catalog is a much larger index in that it is a systematic guide to a group of materials, providing access (guiding you) to the books it includes. A periodicals database is an index that is a guide to the contents of many magazines, journals, and newspapers. A bibliography performs the same way as an index by providing access to citations of materials that are on one subject or by one author. Your library's catalog serves as an index to the books in the library by giving you the information you need to find books on your topic, such as the call numbers and perhaps some information about where in the library building(s) those call numbers are shelved.

After you have searched in a search tool, you use the information you found there to retrieve the actual information resource, like a book or article about your topic. Your next step after using the database would be to determine if your library has the materials that you identified. A full text database makes this task easy because you simply have to click on the appropriate link to see the entire article. You can then print the article, email it to yourself, or read it online. It is important to remember that not all full text databases contain the complete text of every resource for which they have a citation. For example, the database in Figure 2–2 provides full text of only those citations that have the phrase "HTML Full Text," "PDF Full Text," or sometimes "Link to Full Text" with the citation. Many full text databases further contain different graphics than you would see in the print version of the periodical. Other periodicals will not be available full-text even in a full text database because their publishers have set an embargo, a time period of perhaps a year or two, during which their resources may not be digitized. Or perhaps your library simply does not subscribe to the periodical. This means you may have access to the full text of older issues, but not the current issues. In these instances, you may have access only to an article's citation and perhaps its abstract. If your library subscribes to the periodical in its paper version, you can still get the article right away. If your library does not have the periodical in either electronic or paper format, you will need to use Interlibrary Loan services.

Many search tools are now available in college libraries exclusively in their online formats. Some tools are available in both paper and electronic versions, but their number is fairly low. There are only a small number of search tools that come solely in paper. An example of an online-only search tool is the database *Lexis-Nexis,* to which many colleges subscribe. *HAPI,* the *Hispanic American Periodicals Index,* is a good example of a tool that comes both electronically and in paper; many smaller institutions subscribe to the paper version only while research universities may have both formats.

CONCEPT CHECK

Identify three search tools available on your library webpage that are related to your college major.

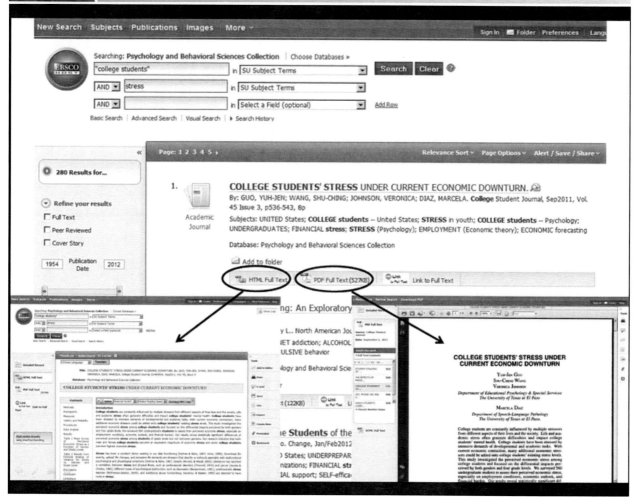

Figure 2-2	A Full-text Article in *Psychology and Behavioral Sciences Collection* Database with Images of HTML Full-text and PDF File (insets)

Screen shot: Copyright © by EBSCO. Reprinted by permission. Excerpts: From *College Student Journal, September 2011, Vol. 45, Issue 3* by Yuh-Jen Guo, Shu-Ching Wang, Veronica Johnson, Marcela Diaz. Copyright © 2011 by Project Innovation. Reprinted by permission.

SELECTING THE BEST SEARCH TOOL(S)

The decision of which tool to use has a tremendous effect on the success of your research. You want to become skilled at relating your topic to a subject field and discipline so that you can select the most appropriate search tool for any given topic. While multidisciplinary search tools are adequate for some general topics, you will be expected to perform more detailed and subject-specific research as you become more knowledgeable about your major.

If you are unsure which search tool to use for your research, look for descriptions of the resources to which the search tool provides access. After reading those descriptions, you can ask yourself several questions:

- Does the search tool provide resources about the time period in which I am interested?
- Does the search tool provide access to the subject or discipline I need?
- Does the search tool cover the right type of resources, such as primary sources or peer-reviewed articles?

Simply put, use the best tool for the job. Be selective about your search tool and you are more likely to retrieve resources that are relevant to your topic.

WHAT DO SEARCH TOOLS CONTAIN?

Search tools contain **references** to information resources. The *American Heritage Dictionary*'s definition of the word reference is "A note in a publication referring the reader to another publication." That is how a search tool provides access; it refers you to the resource that has the information. A search tool consists of references to many resources and each of the references is a **record** that includes information about the resource and often the full text of the resource itself.

Records

Search tools organize information by arranging systematically the records they contain. A record is the description of a resource in a search tool, including books, periodical articles, or sound/video recordings. Records in search tools can also be called references, entries, and citations. These names are interchangeable; they all mean basically the same thing and include the same elements.

Each record contains all the information necessary to enable you to find the item it describes:

- the author(s)
- the title
- the publication information

Each of these elements is contained in its own area in the record. In search tools these areas are called **fields.** Usually the fields are clearly labeled so that you can identify the elements immediately; that is, you can differentiate the title of the article from the title of the periodical in which the article was published. The same elements are present in the records in paper search tools, but they are not usually labeled as fields. Some online search tools display its fields along with their labels, called **field tags,** on the left.

Some examples of field tags include:

SO: means source—the title of the periodical that's the "source" of the article, same meaning as JN.
JN: means journal name—the periodical title, same meaning as SO.
TI: means title. This can be confusing because TI usually refers to the title of the book or article rather than the title of the periodical. However, this field tag varies from tool to tool. You should scan the other fields before you cite the resource or go looking for it in the library.
PY: means publication year—the year that the book or article was published.
AU: means author. Other information, such as an editor or translator, may be included here and must often be included in your citation of the resource.

Citations (full discussion in Chapter 4)

A search tool provides enough information for the researcher to find each information resource, just as you provide your professors when you "cite your sources."

 SEARCH TIP

Many databases provide a Cite This feature allows you to quickly access a citation for use in your bibliography.

The word citation comes from the word cite, which means, "to quote as an authority or example; to mention or bring forward as support, illustration, or proof," according to the *American Heritage Dictionary*. You have probably provided citations for research projects you have done because your instructor required you to cite your sources. These citations can be found in your bibliography or Works Cited page at the end of your research papers. However, these are not the only places where lists of citations appear; they are found with nearly all scholarly research. Periodicals databases are often called bibliographic databases because they are also lists of citations for resources; i.e., bibliographies. Regardless of its location, a citation will always contain the same elements: author, title, and publication information. These three components may be arranged differently depending on the citation style you're using, but the sequence is usually:

1. author(s)
2. title
3. publication information

Search Modes and Search Terms

A **search mode** is a way to use a search tool; that is, it is one way that you can look up something, one mode of searching, in a particular tool. A search mode can also be referred to as an access point. Each search mode, like field searching, provides access to a record. Search modes include title searches, looking through the titles of resources you are trying to find in a catalog; author searches, in which the author's name is searched; and subject searches, using the subject that you type into a database or into a search engine's textbox to find resources. Other search modes may be document-type searches, searches by location, or by the language of the resources. Most search tools allow you to search anything at all in the record; all fields are available. It is often helpful to know which search modes are available in the tool you choose so that you can decide what your search term(s) will be. See Figure 2–3 for a menu of search modes/fields that are options in a periodicals database.

Figure 2–3   Search Mode Options in *Academic Search Complete* Database

A **search term** is the actual word(s) you look up in a search tool. It may be only one word, a phrase of several words, or even a report or document number. Databases allow you to use almost anything as your search mode and search term(s), and most allow combinations of them.

Authors and Titles as Search Terms

Each of the elements in a citation or record is a potential search mode. You are familiar with some search modes if you ever searched in a library's catalog to see if the library has any books by your favorite author, or if you used the catalog to find out if the library has a copy of a book for which your professor gave you only the title. You were using the search modes of author in the first instance and title in the second. Author and title search modes often make research easy because they are yes/no searches: Are there any works in this library by Stephen King? Does the library have *The Hunger Games?*

In the title search mode most search tools allow you to enter any word from a title as your search term and to specify that you are looking for it as a word in the title. You may have to be more precise when using the author as a search mode. Some search tools require that you invert the author's name (put the last name first) in an author search. You can check each tool, simply by performing a test search, to find out if any search mode requires a specified format.

How Search Tools Differ

Because most tools are now online, the main difference among them is the amount of information provided in the records. Library catalogs generally furnish citations that include the title of a book, its author(s), and the publishing information. Many also provide a link to the online version of the resource if it is available in that format.

Periodicals databases also provide author, title, and publication information for the articles they list. A database citation includes the periodical title, volume, and date because you need all this information to cite the article or to locate it elsewhere. Most databases also supply an **abstract**, a brief summary of the cited item. If the database is not completely full text, the abstract enables you to evaluate a resource before you see the full text. Regardless of whether the article's full text is available, the abstract helps you decide at an early point in your research if the resource is relevant to your topic and therefore worth printing or tracking down. Figure 2–4a shows a database entry for a journal article that includes the citation only, while Figure 2–4b shows another record from the same tool that includes an abstract.

"Relevance" Rankings

It is important to remember that the database does not evaluate the materials retrieved. You have simply instructed the search tool to retrieve any record that has your search terms included in the results. Some databases and search engines list the webpages they retrieve by relevance. How each search engine determines relevance may differ, but it is generally based on how often your search

 SEARCH TIP

Read the abstract of an article before clicking Print! You may discover it won't be helpful to your research.

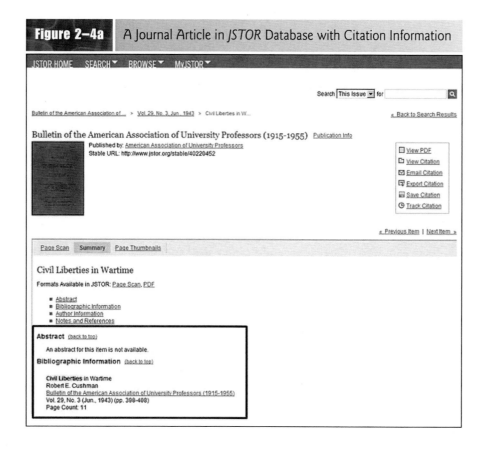

Figure 2–4a   A Journal Article in *JSTOR* Database with Citation Information

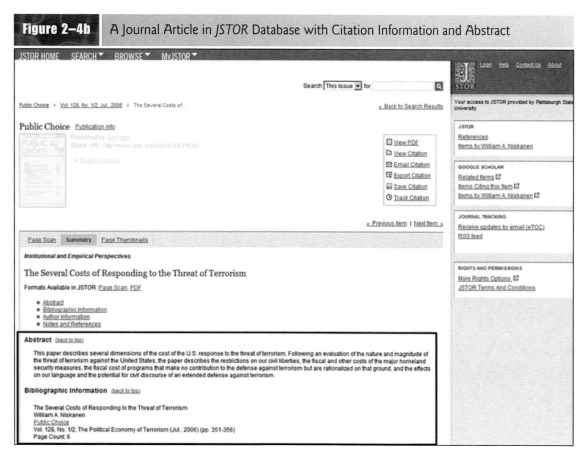

Figure 2–4b   A Journal Article in *JSTOR* Database with Citation Information and Abstract

term appears in the webpage or database record, how long the webpage has existed, and the number of other webpages that link to the page. Note that the high frequency of your search term does not guarantee that the resource in which it is used is relevant or reliable. Web searches become even more problematic when your search term is a common word or has several definitions or uses. In these cases, irrelevant results are commonplace. Library databases may be a better choice since they provide mechanisms, like search modes, by which you can more easily narrow your search to relevant results.

ANALYZING YOUR TOPIC AND USING THE WEB

The ease with which *Google* provides millions of results on your topic may lead you to believe that you do not need to know your topic's subject field or discipline. You may assume you just type your topic into the search box and let it "find stuff" for you. Research shows, however, that many students go no further than the first screen or two of webpages retrieved in the search. The problem with this approach is that it is highly likely that the search engine will deliver an overwhelming amount of information to you, unsorted in any way that is useful to you.

You can improve your research on the Web by using the Web to give you an idea of your topic's scope or its related sub-fields. In those cases you are using a search engine as you would an encyclopedia—to begin your research. However, because there is so much information accessible on the Web, this approach will take some time. If you do find an interesting angle through this approach, you will probably want to investigate your narrowed topic using a variety of search tools, taking care to evaluate the information you find. It is also important to remember that databases consider the word(s) you typed to be nothing more than a pattern of data to be searched. The software simply scans through the text of every one of the database's records to find a match for the data you entered. It then compiles a set of every record in which it found a match with your search term, and it displays this list of results. You must use your own evaluative criteria to select those results from the list that are appropriate to your needs.

Regardless of where you search, the search term you use is a term that you think describes your research topic. Yet the database often retrieves records that seem to be completely unrelated to the topic, both in databases and on the Web. This typically occurs because it is searching for a pattern of data you entered and not searching for a subject. That data-pattern, which you perceive as a word or phrase, is somewhere in every record it retrieves. You need to learn how to make your

CONCEPT CHECK

Perform a search for *AIDS* in a periodicals database. Notice the variety of subjects this search retrieves. Suggest a more precise term for the subject in which you are interested.

◆ SEARCH TIP

The search tool does not actually think or make decisions for you; rather it simply matches data, in this case words, and collects those matches for you.

search more focused so that the database retrieves more of what you want. You do that by using a clear search statement.

SEARCH TERMS

Controlled Vocabulary

Some disciplines require specific terminology to precisely describe a topic or technique. Databases often reflect this specific terminology to provide precision in searching. This is known as a **controlled vocabulary.** The result is that a subject will always be found under the same "approved" term, making the search for a subject easier and more successful. If you do not use this controlled vocabulary, you will retrieve results, but perhaps not complete results and perhaps not the best results. A database does not index resources about date rape under *date rape* one day, and on another day index them under *acquaintance rape,* and on yet another day index them under *violence in dating situations.* A controlled vocabulary limits the potential search terms to the one approved term a particular database uses to describe that topic. You can often find this controlled vocabulary in an article's Descriptor field. It may appear that there is only one approved term to describe your topic, but this is not necessarily the case. Different databases may use different controlled vocabulary.

Natural Language (Uncontrolled Vocabulary)

How many terms for *drunkenness* would you actually use in a search tool to look for information on this condition? Probably not many. Your list is an example of natural language, one that uses any number of words and terms for the same concept. Your "unofficial" list, the one that includes slang and everyday terminology, is significantly longer than the list of "approved" terms you would use in research. The list of terms you think of as "approved" includes terms that are more formal than those in your own vocabulary list. These formal terms are used in serious discussions of a subject or in more scholarly resources. When doing research it is useful to search for terms considered Standard English before trying slang or highly technical terms. Searches using this approach often retrieve more relevant results. For instance, you would find that *adolescent pregnancy* is more successful than *unwed teen mothers.* Some of the major advantages to using a tool with a controlled vocabulary are:

- Your search will be more successful. Once you discover the term used by a search tool to describe your topic, you can find all records for resources about that topic under that term in that tool, not just those records that happen to have the word you typed.
- Frequently you can also find closely related terms that describe subjects similar to that of the one term. For example, these three subject headings, *acquaintance rape, date rape,* and *dating violence,* describe subjects that are obviously closely related but not quite the same phenomenon. A well-controlled vocabulary allows for fine distinctions among closely related terms such as this.

 SEARCH TIP

Always make note of a database's suggested search terms.

Figure 2–5	Concept Breakdowns in Sample Topics		
reincarnation	Buddhism		
Thor	Norse	mythology	
preservation	Civil War	battlefields	
credibility	predictions	polar ice melt	global warming

Figure 2–6	Concept Breakdown in *Academic Search Complete* Database's Search Boxes

New Search   Publications   Subject Terms   Cited References   More ⌄

Searching: **Academic Search Complete** | Choose Databases »

preservation   in SU Subject Terms ▼   Search   Clear ⑦

AND ▼ "civil war"   in SU Subject Terms ▼

AND ▼ battlefields   in SU Subject Terms ▼   Add Row

Basic Search | Advanced Search | Visual Search | ▶ Search History

Copyright © by EBSCO. Reprinted by permission.

Search Statements

A **search statement** is simply the words you type that work as a command to the search tool. Formulating a clear search statement helps the tool better locate relevant information on your topic. It is far easier to match a clear idea than a fuzzy one. For an efficient search, you need a clear statement of your information need. The best way to do this is to describe your need as separate concepts. Some examples of topics with several components are:

- Reincarnation in Buddhism
- Role of the god Thor in Norse mythology
- Attempts to preserve civil war battlefields
- Credibility of predictions about polar ice melt from global warming

It is useful to break complex topics into smaller components. One method some researchers use is to create several columns and write the individual concepts that are part of your topic in each column. The sample topics listed above would fall into columns as shown in Figure 2–5.

Note that not all the words from the topics appear to be major concepts. In most cases this is because the omitted words are unnecessary. You would typically include only the major concepts that are necessary to understand the topic. The use of unneeded words will not make a search totally unworkable, but can often unnecessarily decrease the number of results. Figure 2–6 shows how the concepts from one topic breakdown appear in a database search screen. Almost every topic can be disassembled into its concepts, and good topics nearly always have more than one concept. A general rule is that a one-concept topic is not usually appropriate for college-level research.

Figure 2–7	Concept Breakdown with Synonyms	
		Reincarnation
Buddhism		Afterlife
		the hereafter
		eternal life

| Figure 2–8 | Concept Breakdown with Synonyms in an *Academic Search Complete* Database Search |

Copyright © by EBSCO. Reprinted by permission.

Once you have broken your topic's concepts into columns, you can determine synonyms for those concepts, as shown in Figure 2–7. Synonyms allow you to make your topic flexible by allowing you to add or subtract terms from revised search statements as you encounter too much or too little information.

If your first search using *Buddhism* and *reincarnation,* for example, brought back too few resources, you could expand your search by telling the database to search instead for *Buddhism* and *afterlife.* The same could be done with the other synonyms listed in Figure 2–7. **Adding synonyms to a search statement broadens a search.** It requires the database to bring back all matches for all terms. Explanatory discussion of how to accomplish these multiple searches in only one search follows later in the chapter.

You can enter synonyms into separate textboxes in a database's search form. Be sure to use the OR option when doing this as in Figure 2–8. The use of and difference between AND and OR, the basic commands for database searches, are discussed later in the chapter.

CONCEPT CHECK

How many synonyms are there for the word "drunkenness?"

Figure 2-9	Adding a Concept to Narrow a Search

	reincarnation	
Buddhism	afterlife	Karma
	the hereafter	
	eternal life	

Figure 2-10	Adding a Concept to Narrow an *Academic Search Complete* Database Search

New Search | Publications | Subject Terms | Cited References | More ˅

Searching: **Academic Search Complete** | Choose Databases »

Buddhism — in [SU Subject Terms ▼] [Search] [Clear] ?

AND ▼ reincarnation — in [AB Abstract or Author-Supplied Abstrac ▼]

OR ▼ afterlife — in [AB Abstract or Author-Supplied Abstrac ▼]

OR ▼ hereafter — in [AB Abstract or Author-Supplied Abstrac ▼]

AND ▼ karma — in [AB Abstract or Author-Supplied Abstrac ▼]   Add Row | Remove Row

Basic Search | Advanced Search | Visual Search | ▶ Search History

If the topic *Buddhism* and *reincarnation* (and its synonyms) yielded too many items for you to skim through you might add another concept. Perhaps you could focus on the role that *karma* plays, if any, in the idea of reincarnation. Your search would then become the statement illustrated in Figure 2–9. **Adding concepts to a search statement narrows or refocuses a search.** It requires the database to retrieve only items that include your specified concepts/terms, as illustrated in Figure 2–10.

You are able to broaden the search by adding synonyms into any column. Perhaps *destiny* and *fate* could be "OR-ed" with *karma*.

Remember that a search tool does nothing intuitively. You have to tell the search tool explicitly which concepts you need and you do this by typing the search terms for the concepts. The

SKILL CHECK

Search the abstract field for the term *spousal abuse* in two different databases. Examine the Descriptor field in several articles related to this topic. How does the terminology related to *spousal abuse* differ between the two databases?

search tool does not know exactly what you are looking for and it sees no meaning in the search terms you interpret as meaningful words. To create the best searches it is necessary to understand the mechanics of how to create sets. You can create sets using Boolean logic. **A set is a group of items retrieved from a search.** Items in each set are records for articles or book chapters in a database, or webpages found by a search engine. A database search using a single word, such as *Inca*, would result in one set including all articles in which the word *Inca* appears.

BOOLEAN LOGIC AND BOOLEAN SEARCHING

When to Use Boolean Operators

Do you always have to use Boolean searching? The simple answer is no. This is partly because of the implicit use of operators by databases and Web search engines, and partly because you may be using a term that is distinctive enough to retrieve relevant hits through a simple search. For example, when searching for a topic such as *stem cell research* a student could enter that phrase into a database search form with no further elaboration, retrieving records on the topic. The database would search for *stem* AND *cell* AND *research* by default. You could focus the search more by adding a concept, *ethics,* using Boolean operators. Your search statement would then become *stem* AND *cell* AND *research* AND *ethics,* and it would retrieve fewer items which include all four concepts.

Surprisingly, sometimes terms that appear to be distinctive enough to retrieve a focused set of materials turn out to be much broader. Take for example, the specific-sounding term *cloning.* Searching for that term in a general database without specifying a field retrieves 34,817 records. Even limiting the search to the Subject field retrieves 15,600 records. How can you narrow your search so that you can look through a manageable amount of records? Add additional concepts. Focus your search on *cloning* (AND *embryo**) and you will have to select your relevant articles from 1,233 records. Clearly, you must continue to add search terms to retrieve a useful number of results. A further demonstration of the need for a second concept was a similar simple search in *Google.* Searching for *cloning* retrieved over 38,600,000 hits! Adding the term *embryo* dropped that to 5,750,000.

Searching for information is becoming more complicated all the while it is becoming easier. This may be because there is so much more information available than ever before. Another reason is the continuous evolution of information technology. Keep in mind that your brain is still more complex than the technology you use for research. Thinking before you "type something in" is the best way to get only as much information as you need.

Databases and Web search engines use Boolean logic in a technique known as **Boolean searching** to sort through records and create sets, matching terms in your search statement. Remember that databases were created as mathematical machines originally. Boolean logic is a mathematical approach to retrieving information. How does "Boolean" work?

Boolean searching uses **Boolean operators** to include only the records that match your search terms correctly. Boolean searching is the default for most databases and search engines. The three operators are commands that look like regular words: AND, OR, and NOT.

■   **AND** is the most commonly used operator. It requires the search tool to create a final set that contains *all* terms that were typed by the researcher. Thus, the search term *South American prehistory* requires that all items in the final set include *South* AND *American* AND *prehistory.* Thus **AND narrows a search: it decreases the number of records in the final set.**

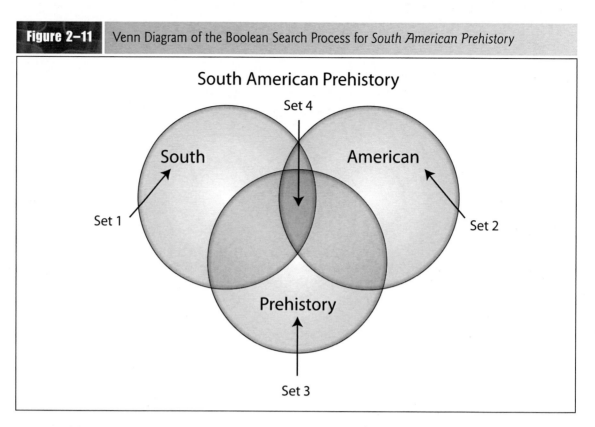

Figure 2–11   Venn Diagram of the Boolean Search Process for *South American Prehistory*

Figure 2–12   Pizza Toppings Illustrating Boolean Operators

The "Venn diagram" in Figure 2–11 demonstrates a database using AND to retrieve all items that included all search words: *South* AND *American* AND *prehistory*. Only Set 4 includes articles with all three search terms.

The other Boolean operators are used less frequently than AND, especially since search programs began to use AND implicitly (without stating that fact). All the Boolean operators are still powerful tools and an information literate researcher is able to put them to use.

- ■ **OR** commands the search tool to retrieve *all* items that have ANY of the terms that were typed by the researcher. When using OR the researcher wants the records that include any of her search terms. Thus **OR broadens a search; it increases the number of results.**

The searches in Figure 2–12 illustrate the work of Boolean operators OR and AND with the (imaginary) toppings on a pizza. Think of ordering a pizza. You might want a pepperoni pizza or a vegetarian pizza. Your friend may want a Hawaiian pizza with ham and pineapple. When you call to order your pizza, you will use Boolean logic.

Searches using only OR will create sets that include *any* record that has *any* of the search terms. A search that "OR-ed" together many synonyms could have a very large number of records in its final set. The set retrieved in an information search using the Boolean operator AND will include only those records that include *all* the terms that have been "AND-ed" together in a search statement.

The difference between AND and OR may seem somewhat counterintuitive. Some researchers have a tendency to use OR to try to retrieve fewer records and AND to retrieve more, when a skilled researcher knows to use the two operators in a completely opposite manner.

■ **NOT** is the least used operator. It sometimes appears on search pages as the option "AND NOT." It must be used very carefully so as not to exclude items that may have your other search terms as well as the one NOT wanted. You want an "Everything" pizza and not anchovies. Use NOT to avoid false hits from search terms that have multiple meanings. For example, use NOT when searching for articles on apple (fruit) crops to "NOT-out" articles on Apple databases. Your search statement would be *apples* NOT *databases*. But use NOT with caution. **NOT excludes items from search results.**

Boolean operators allow the database to find all or any of your search terms, depending on which operator(s) you use.

An example of a college-level topic searched using Boolean operators is *embryonic stem cell research for cures to Parkinson's disease*. If you connect the two concepts with OR, as in Figure 2-13a, the search would produce one set of results with all entries containing either of the search terms. The articles on Parkinson's disease would be about all aspects of that disease from

| Figure 2–13a | Search Using OR |

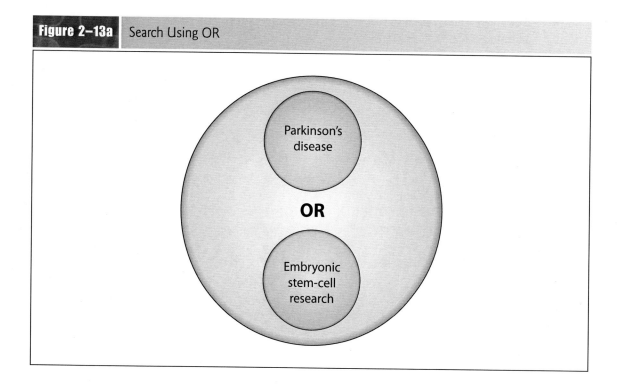

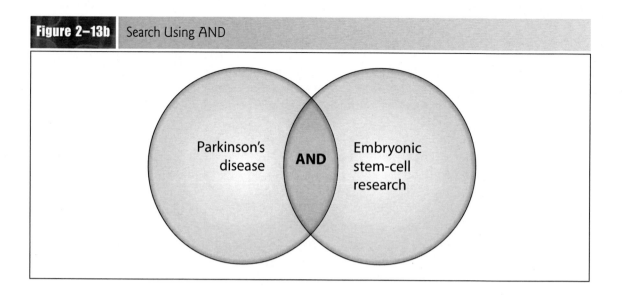

Figure 2-13b Search Using AND

Parkinson's disease | AND | Embryonic stem-cell research

Figure 2-14 An Entry in the List of Websites Retrieved in a *Google* Search

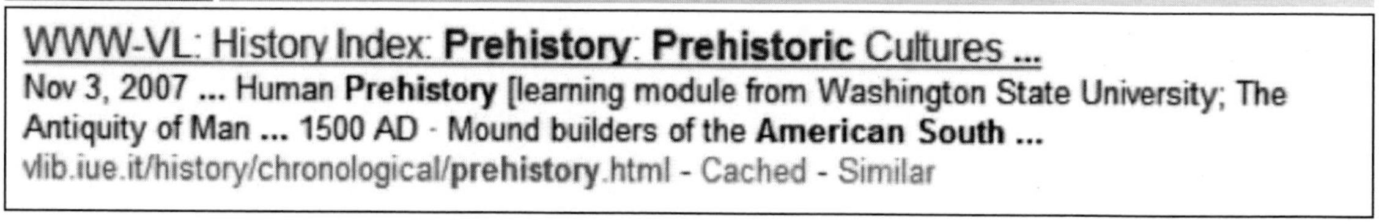

WWW-VL: History Index: **Prehistory**: **Prehistoric** Cultures ...
Nov 3, 2007 ... Human **Prehistory** [learning module from Washington State University; The Antiquity of Man ... 1500 AD - Mound builders of the **American South ...**
vlib.iue.it/history/chronological/**prehistory**.html - Cached - Similar

drug therapies to brain-scans. Some of the articles would be about using embryonic stem cells. The articles about embryonic stem cell research would also be about all aspects of that concept from how to harvest the cells to legislation about research funding. Some of these articles would be about Parkinson's disease.

When you connect the terms with AND, the search retrieves a smaller number of articles, but all items have both search terms. This is the "boxed set" depicted in Figure 2–13b that includes all the search terms.

Implicit Boolean Searches and Phrases as Search Terms

Many databases use both implicit (unstated and therefore invisible) and explicit (visible) Boolean logic when performing searches. Most search engines use implicit Boolean logic in their basic searches when matching phrases typed by researchers. Implicit Boolean searching means the program defaults to searching for all the words typed by the researcher. *Google* states in its Basic Search Help page: "Describe what you need with as few terms as possible. The goal of each word in a query is to focus it further. Since all words are used, each additional word limits the results." *Google* **automatically assumes there is a Boolean AND between all words** you enter, so you don't need to include 'and' between terms.

Implicit Boolean searching (all words in any order) could mean that one result of the earlier search for materials on *South American prehistory* would include information resources that deal with the American South's prehistory, which is quite different from what the researcher had in mind. As seen in Figure 2–14 one of the items on the first page of retrieved webpages in a *Google* search is not relevant.

| Figure 2–15 | Phrase-Searching on the *Google* Advanced Search Page |

Google

Advanced Search

Find pages with...		To do this in the search box
all these words:		Type the important words: `tricolor rat terrier`
this exact word or phrase:		Put exact words in quotes: `"rat terrier"`
any of these words:		Type OR between all the words you want: `miniature OR standard`
none of these words:		Put a minus sign just before words you don't want: `-rodent, -"Jack Russell"`

One easy technique to specify word order is to use quotation marks to search for phrases. Materials retrieved in such a search should be only those that use the *phrase:* i.e., only materials including "South American prehistory" *in that order.*

Some databases and search engines offer phrase-searching as an option in a menu on their Advanced Search pages. You may select "all words," "any words," or "the exact phrase." This is sometimes called *adjacency.* See Figure 2–15 for an example of these options on *Google*'s Advanced Search page.

Be sure to check the "Search Tips" or "Help" button when first using a tool that is new to you; it saves you time. Then, always scan the results screen for additional search options and navigational features.

FIELD-SPECIFIC SEARCHING

Searching a limited number of fields is another good way to focus the search. Many databases retain the keyword search default on their Basic Search pages, but most Advanced Search pages offer a variety of fields to search. See Figure 2–16 for an example of a drop-down menu of many different search fields in one database. The field(s) you select to search can drastically affect your search results. Searches in a general database under the search term *global warming* resulted in the following numbers of records:

- 74,281 when using the All Text field
- 19,043 when using the Abstract field
- 15,167 when using the Subject Terms field

The default field in this case is a good one in which to start a broad search; however, a popular topic such as *global warming* will require adding additional search terms in order to further narrow the results.

Searching the All Text field above retrieved the greatest number of records because the search words simply had to be present in a record. This provides results similar to a *Google* search.

An abstract is a brief summary of the content of an information resource. An abstract, therefore, should include terms that are important in the content of the article. If your database is not defaulted to search the abstract field, you may want to select it from the field menu if you can.

Figure 2–16	A Menu of Searchable Fields in *Academic Search Complete* Database

Copyright © by EBSCO. Reprinted by permission.

Searching the Subject field yielded the fewest but likely the most relevant records, because all records had to be *about* global warming.

Other relevant fields such as Author, Title, and Source similarly allow you to narrow your results. Many other limiter options are also available. Limiters, also known as facets, allow you to further narrow your results by criteria such as Document Type, Language, Date, Scholarly/Peer-Reviewed, and Full Text. See Figure 2–17 for an illustration of limiters.

For example, if your professor requires an assignment where you must find a research article from a peer-reviewed journal, you could use the subject field to retrieve a relevant research article and combine that with peer-reviewed article as a limiter to further narrow the results. If you did not limit your search to peer-reviewed sources, you would retrieve many results unacceptable for the assignment, such as book reviews and magazine articles.

This is only one search tip to remember as you do more searches. Using search tools is a learning process. You will get better with experience.

Subject searching is another type of field searching where the use of controlled vocabulary is especially helpful. It may be familiar to you already. You have used it in an index in a book, or in a catalog in a library, or in a search engine on the Web. You wanted to find information about something, so you looked up the subject or topic you were researching. You can assume that there are

CONCEPT CHECK

Select a popular database at your library and review that database's field searching options. Name the database you chose and five fields in which you can search.

Figure 2-17 Limiters in *Academic Search Complete* Database

usually synonyms for your initial search terms that will yield more information resources. How can you do the most thorough search? It may be necessary to find the terms for your subject that are employed by the search tools you are using.

SUBJECT HEADINGS, TAGS, AND FACETS

Information is often organized by subject. Librarians, editors, or publishers examine the contents of an information resource (a book or a periodical or newspaper article or a videotape) and decide what the resource is about. In a library, a catalog librarian assigns to the resource, most often a book, a small number of subject headings that describe the resource's content. At a database company, the process is very similar: The indexer assigns to an information resource several terms that describe its subject content. **These terms may be called subject headings, keywords, tags, facets, or descriptors.**

Once the resource has been assigned its terms, those become searchable parts of the record. The work of the catalogers and indexers make it possible for you to use subject as a search mode: Descriptors/tags/keywords/facets/subject headings are search modes in many search tools. You can also search under your own search terms, but usually you will be more successful—get a higher percentage of relevant results—when you use the tool's controlled vocabulary for your subject.

You can command the tool to search for almost any access point in one field or in all fields. Let's say you want to search a library's catalog for George Orwell's novel, *1984*. You can command the database software to search all fields (very often this is the default search mode) or to search only the title field for it. The latter is a "field-specific search" because it commands the database to scan for a match in only the field you selected. Such a strategy eliminates the possibility of finding unwanted matches that have *1984* in their publication-year fields; that field was not scanned because you opted to look in the title field only. There usually are on-screen suggestions for field-specific searches, most often a small downward arrow indicating a drop-down menu of fields, as depicted in Figure 2–18. A database's method for allowing field-specific searches will change from tool to tool, as will the fields from which you may choose. It is necessary, therefore, to explore the fields available in the tools you wish to use.

Figure 2–18   A Menu of Fields in *WorldCat* Database

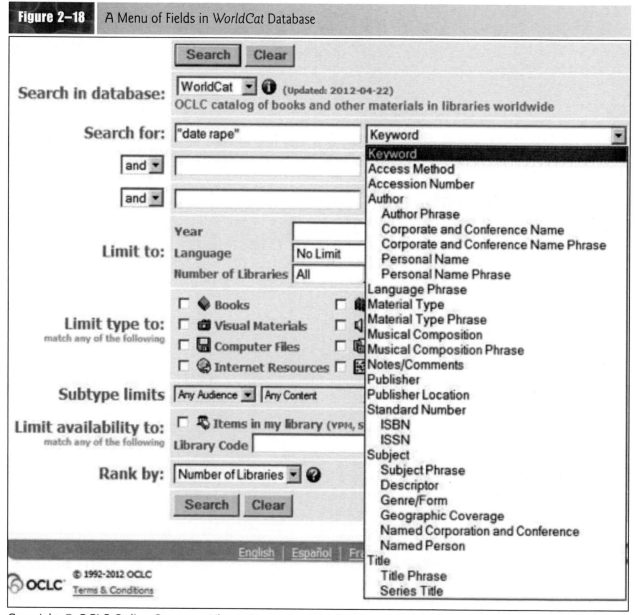

SEARCHING TOPICS EFFECTIVELY

Not all topics work equally well in all search tools. You can almost always find something on a topic by simply typing it into *Google*. But chances are that the first screen of webpages, which is the number of screens that most students glance over, will not include the best webpage for your information need. Chances of getting relevant scholarly results are greater when you do a search in a database, especially if you selected an appropriate one whose scope includes your topic. Besides using quotation marks to search for a phrase and taking advantage of appropriate search fields, you can also search your topic more effectively by using Boolean logic.

As stated earlier, almost all search tools use an implicit Boolean function. There is no need for this powerful approach when you are searching very broadly, usually at the beginning of your research. As your focus narrows you will need to retrieve more materials focused on a more specific aspect of the broad topic. Retrieving multiple focused resources (as discussed earlier in Planning Your Research), will allow you to more easily weave the different aspects of your topic into one cohesive research paper. Let's look at your topic one more time.

Most topics include more than one concept. This means that a topic that sounds simple is actually a bit more complex. One example is the topic of synthetic drugs. A simple search for synthetic drugs would likely produce results on a wide variety of subtopics. A focused search using Boolean operators will give you more closely related results. This is illustrated with the research question "In what ways do synthetic drugs affect mental status?" This research question has two main concepts that must be linked: synthetic drugs and mental status. You can locate the main topic by deleting all the "tiny" words, such as articles, prepositions, and conjunctions, from your research question, as in this example:

~~In what ways do~~ synthetic drugs ~~affect~~ mental status?

Though it sounds contradictory, you can do a focused search that is expanded by using synonyms. You can connect synonyms using the Boolean operator OR the synonyms you listed beneath one another in columns; you connect their concepts—the separate columns—with AND. See Figure 2–19.

~~In what ways do~~ synthetic drugs ~~affect~~ mental status?

Figure 2–19	Concepts and Synonyms with Boolean Operators	
Synthetic drugs	AND	mental status
OR		OR
K2		mental health
OR		OR
Spice		mood
OR		OR
Bath salts		wellness

 SEARCH TIP

Think of what a tool is used for before you use it. Is it the most appropriate for your topic?

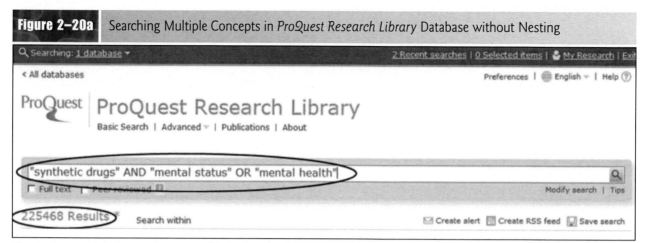

Figure 2–20a   Searching Multiple Concepts in *ProQuest Research Library* Database without Nesting

The images and their contents are published with permission of ProQuest LLC. Further reproduction is prohibited without permission.

New researchers often attempt to improve a search by adding more words to it. This works only if the added words are *synonyms* for the concepts already there. If a researcher adds a concept the search narrows. For example, searching for information on *women in the military* using the search *women* AND *military* retrieved 3,518 records. By adding *combat* into the search which then becomes *women* AND *military* AND *combat,* the number of records dropped to 336. Conversely, dropping a concept will broaden a search, so that when a student searches for information on *meningitis* AND *college students* AND *women* and gets only 1 record, you can drop *college students* from the search and retrieve 41 records. These examples show how you can use your results to refine your search.

Nested Search Terms

As stated earlier, researchers can have trouble using the Boolean operators AND and OR effectively. Notice the search statement circled in Figure 2–20a. Multiple concepts are being searched. In an explicit Boolean search the parentheses command the search tool in the same way they organize mathematical functions in a formula.

The search in Figure 2–20a is a good example of the database making no decisions for the user: Which function should be performed first? Is it a search for all articles on *synthetic drugs* AND *mental status* with all the articles on *mental health* as well? Or is it a search for all articles on either *mental status* OR *mental health* selected from articles on *synthetic drugs* (by AND-ing)? Your experience with mathematical statements (e.g., $4 \times 2 + 98$), will help you understand the situation: Is it $4 \times 2 (= 8) + 98$, or $2 + 98 (= 100) \times 4$? Remember that the database is performing a mathematical function when it's searching and it can be commanded in a similar way, with parentheses. You would use parentheses to "nest" each math function that must be performed; e.g., multiply 4 times 2 and then add 98 in a mathematical formula becomes $(4 \times 2) + 98$. Next, examine the circled search statement in Figure 2–20b and the search results (in the circle) from using nested search terms; i.e., using parentheses.

Note that the number of items retrieved is far smaller in the second search. The search in Figure 2–20a retrieved 225,468 records, while the search in Figure 2–20b retrieved 78 records. The reason for the difference is the clearer focus of the matches sought by the search program.

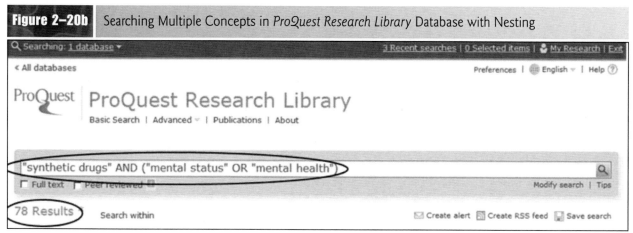

Figure 2–20b Searching Multiple Concepts in *ProQuest Research Library* Database with Nesting

The images and their contents are published with permission of ProQuest LLC. Further reproduction is prohibited without permission.

Parenthetical nesting can also help searches on the Web, just be sure to check your Web search engine's protocols for using Boolean operators. In this type of search a concept and its synonyms should be enclosed in parentheses using OR, and then the parenthetical statements are "AND-ed" together.

Truncating Search Terms

Another technique that can help your searching is called **truncation.** This technique **allows the search tool to search for a "root word" by itself or with any/all endings.** It is sometimes called wild card searching. It is a technique that addresses problems often faced by researchers: Should I search for a singular or plural version of my term? Am I sure I have spelled my search term correctly? What if the noun form looks very different from the adjective form? For example, a search for a topic about *teenagers* needs to retrieve documents that use the words *teen, teens, teenage, teenager,* and *teenagers.* Many search tools now default to searching for variants of the search term and may retrieve materials that include any of those variants. Some databases are not yet that flexible; many search automatically only for simple plural forms. In such databases, how do you enter all the variants other than plurals that you want to look for? For example, must you type all relevant terms to retrieve all relevant materials because the tool will search for only one of those forms otherwise? What can you do for terms that may have many variants? You can use *truncation.* Most

CONCEPT CHECK

By using your favorite search engine's Advanced Search option, you can see if it's one that offers the option to use explicit Boolean searching.

Figure 2–21	Help Screens for Truncation in *ProQuest Research Library*

Search Tips
Searching > Search Tips

Wildcards and truncation
You can use wildcards and truncation when you're looking for documents that contain spelling variants, or words that begin with the same character string.

Character	Description	Example
?	Wildcard character - used to replace any single character, either inside or at the right end of a word. Multiple wildcards can be used to represent multiple characters.	**nurse?** Finds: nurses, nursed, but not nurse **sm?th** Finds: smith and smyth **ad???** Finds: added, adult, adopt
*	**Truncation character** (*) - retrieves variations of the search term. Use the truncation character at the beginning (left-hand truncation), the end (right-hand truncation) or in the middle of search terms. Each truncated word can return up to 500 word variations. **Standard truncation** (*) retrieves variations on the search term, replacing up to 10 characters. **Defined truncation** ([*n] or $n) replaces up to the number of characters specified, for example [*50]. The maximum number of characters that can be entered is 125.	**nurse*** Finds: nurse, nurses, nursed **colo*r** Finds: colour, color ***old** Finds: told, household, bold **[*5]beat** Finds: upbeat, downbeat, offbeat, heartbeat
$n or [*n]	$n and [*n] are equivalent operators used to denote up to how many characters you want to truncate.	**nutr$5, nutr[*5]** Finds: nutrition, nutrient, nutrients

The images and their contents are published with permission of ProQuest LLC. Further reproduction is prohibited without permission.

databases allow this technique and explain it in their "Help" sections. Figure 2–21 provides an example of how *ProQuest Research Library* includes information about its truncation symbols via its Help screen.

Use the truncation symbol specified—* or ?, etc.—by the database you're using. For example, search under *latin** and you retrieve records that include the words *latin, latins, latin's, latino, latinos, latina, latinas,* or *latin_ _ _* (any other ending). This technique is especially helpful with punctuation such as apostrophes: Is it Asperger syndrome or Asperger's syndrome? Type your search as *asperger** and you are covered either way!

Truncation is not recommended when searching the Web. Common sense tells you why: The number of webpages retrieved would swamp your database if ANY form of a search term were included on each page.

CHAPTER HIGHLIGHTS

- Search tools provide access to information because they consist of references to information resources such as books and periodical articles.

- Search tools include catalogs, periodicals databases, bibliographies, and search engines.

- Information in search tools is organized into records that are also called citations, entries, and references.

- A record in a search tool is made up of fields that together contain enough information to enable you to find the actual resource: author, title, and publishing information, each in its own field(s) in the record. Many records in full text databases also include the full contents of the information resource itself.

- A search mode offers you different ways to use a search tool. A search term is the word or phrase or number you look up.

- The scope of a search tool or an information resource can be subject-oriented, discipline-oriented, or general.

- The subject field/discipline relationship in information systems allows you to broaden or narrow your research by using more- or less-focused tools and resources to get information on your topic.

- Selecting the best search tool for the topic is a critical decision early in your research.

- Understanding the concepts in a topic makes it both focused and flexible, so that the researcher retrieves a high percentage of records that truly address her information needs.

- Breaking a topic into its component concepts allows you to use the power of the search tool's matching skills. A researcher may write out the concepts in columns, putting synonyms in a list under the appropriate concept.

- Focused research pays off because it results in information resources that are clearly related to the topic you consciously selected and to each other, making your "connecting the dots" of information in the resources easier when you write your paper.

- Boolean logic is a mathematical concept that is applied to information searching. Boolean searching employs the Boolean operators AND, OR, and NOT to manipulate items in the sets of records retrieved.

- AND narrows a search because it requires that all records in the final set include all search terms that were connected with AND. OR broadens a search because it creates sets of records that include *any* of the synonyms or closely related search terms that are connected with OR. NOT excludes records from a search.

■ Many search tools use "implicit Boolean" methods to search for terms when more than one word is included in the search term, unless the searcher uses quotation marks to enclose a multi-word phrase.

■ Subject terms in search tools can be called subject headings or descriptors. They describe the contents of information resources.

■ Subject headings/descriptors are often part of a controlled vocabulary system by which a search tool (usually a catalog or a database) limits the number of terms it uses to describe a topic.

■ Most search tools have drop-down menus that allow the researcher to select which field to search so the database searches more precisely. Field searches are often more successful than keyword or all-fields searches.

■ Search statements benefit from nesting search terms—synonyms that are OR-ed together are enclosed within parentheses—just as mathematical functions work best with nested commands.

■ The addition of a second concept, AND-ing it with the first concept, will usually narrow a search and result in a higher rate of relevant records retrieved.

■ The removal of a concept that had been AND-ed into the search statement will result in a broader search with a greater number of records retrieved.

■ Truncation is a helpful technique that allows searching for a root word with any ending by using a truncation symbol, usually an asterisk (*).

CHAPTER 2

Questions

1. You go to a library at a college you are visiting and it has a library catalog whose records look different from those in your own college's library catalog. What fields would you expect to find in both catalogs' records?

2. Use the topic *juvenile delinquents* to illustrate a controlled vocabulary system. Create a list of terms that might be used to describe the topic, and then search several databases to identify which search terms are used by different databases.

Your Terms	Database Terms

3. Turn the topics below into effective search statements using Boolean operators, truncation, and nesting components when appropriate.

    a.   Why did William Wallace become a symbol of Scotland's struggle for independence?

    b.   Compare nineteenth century and twenty-first century depictions of vampires in popular culture.

    c.   How did the 1845 Irish potato famine affect immigration rates to the United States?

Evaluating

- Examine and compare information from various sources in order to evaluate reliability, validity, accuracy, authority, timeliness, and point of view or bias
- Recognize prejudice, deception, or manipulation
- Describe how the age of a source or the qualities characteristic of the time in which it was created may impact its value
- Describe how the purpose for which information was created affects its usefulness

You have discovered that there is an ocean of information on almost any research topic. This ocean can lead to a feeling of being overwhelmed with information, which is sometimes called information overload. You can prevent information overload by selectively applying evaluative criteria. This chapter will focus on the most critical actions that you will repeat many times during research: evaluation and selection. Evaluation allows you to sift through research results and then select the best research tools and resources for your needs.

You can learn and apply evaluation techniques for the multiple phases of research covered in this textbook: planning your research, doing the research, and integrating research results into your paper or project.

EVALUATING WHILE PLANNING

In the planning phase of research your evaluation tasks are to begin thinking about the information characteristics that will best suit your research assignment/project/paper or personal information need. Think about the requirements of your assignment or information research ideas. What types of information are you likely to need?

If, for example, you need to write a college paper taking a position on a social issues topic such as government managed health care, you should plan to gather information that will:

- Reflect several years of research and long term study of the topic
- Cover the topic from multiple perspectives and viewpoints
- Provide scholarly research suitable for a college paper
- Provide enough detail so that you can form your own opinion

Alternatively, if you are working on a personal project such as researching the best movie to go to with your college roommate, you might want to gather information that includes:

- The most current and up-to-date movie options
- Professional movie reviews and ratings
- Personal opinions from friends or online blogs of people you trust

Clearly, these research projects require different research approaches and the use of different selection criteria when reviewing search results. Planning how you will select your search tools based on an awareness of what types of information will best suit your needs will give you an advantage. Thinking about the type of results you need ahead of time is one sign of an efficient researcher. No matter what your project, planning ahead includes applying early evaluation criteria.

EVALUATING WHILE USING SEARCH TOOLS

You should evaluate the information that you are finding consistently during your research. This is a process that can save you time later. It means you will not print useless articles or retrieve resources that you cannot really use. It may also save you money, or at least paper (and therefore trees), when you decide what to print from a full text database or from the Web. How can you evaluate while researching? You can use the information in search tools themselves to evaluate the resources they cite—before you ever print, or find and copy the references.

You want each of your information resources to be relevant to your topic and authoritative in its subject field. You can best determine this by examining the resource itself. But to avoid going to the stacks for books that are of little relevance, or downloading Web sites that aren't authoritative, or printing or waiting to photocopy articles that are too technical for your needs, you can look at the entries in a search tool for clues to help cull out resources you do not want to pursue. Author and title fields can help you easily evaluate potential information resources.

Using the Title Field to Evaluate a Resource

Take the title first. A title often has a word or a phrase in it that can help you determine the relevance of the resource to your topic. Usually scholarly resources have subtitles with their titles to explain further what the resource is about. You can often decide if a resource fits the scope of your topic by carefully reading its whole title in a search tool. The titles below are similar titles for different books; notice how the subtitle, or lack of one, affects your ability to estimate each book's focus.

> *African Folk Medicine: Practices and Beliefs of the Bambara and Other Peoples*
> *American Folk Medicine*
> *Folk Medicine*
> *Folk Medicine: A Chapter in the History of Culture*
> *Folk Medicine: The Art & the Science*

 SEARCH TIP

Use clues in search tools to evaluate resources for their value in your research.

The title field is most often the easiest way to evaluate a resource for its value to your research. A good measure is that if you can comprehend the *title* of a resource you will probably be able to understand the resource's content.

Using the Author Field to Evaluate a Resource

An author can also be indicative of a resource's applicability to your research. The status of an author is not often determined easily at the beginning of your research, especially if the whole subject field is new to you. But as you continue to search for information on your topic you may see one author's name occurring again and again in different search tools. Or you may find the author mentioned in an encyclopedia article as an authority in the field, and then cited in the bibliography of that article. Sometimes you will encounter an author's name as the second or third author of one article and the first author of another. In this case you may have found work by a whole research team and all of the team's authors can now be searched as authorities.

Do not be a passive researcher. Use information provided by the search tool to select information that is truly relevant to your research. Read through a number of the titles that you retrieve in your research BEFORE you print any of the resources. Be selective! Do a preliminary evaluation of an information resource when you find the first references to it and you will save yourself a lot of time and paper when you go to the printer or to the book stacks, or when you consider whether to request the material from a different library through interlibrary loan. Not everything retrieved by a computer is always relevant.

ACCESS TO "INVISIBLE" INFORMATION

Earlier in this textbook there are examples of records from databases. Databases such as these are part of the invisible Web. According to Bright Planet, an invisible web search company:

> *"The Surface Web, crawled by today's popular search engines, contains only a fraction of the overall unstructured content available on-line today. Surface search results themselves are based on "relevancy by popularity" and ranked by total "hits" by users' simple search queries. Traditional search engines cannot "see" or retrieve content in the Deep Web, which by definition is dynamic content served up in real time from a database in response to a direct query."*

The invisible Web is comprised of pages that are invisible to search engines because the companies that provide the databases make their pages accessible only to paying subscribers. Your library is one of the paying subscribers. There are also online newspapers and periodicals that may provide some of their content to the casual Web surfer but make their archives of past issues available only

SEARCH TIP

An author whose name appears often in your research is probably an authority.

SEARCH TIP

Print or save or scan only citations or articles and websites that are worth reading and citing!

to those who pay for a subscription or by the article. The savvy researcher knows that an older article may well be available full text through a full text database the library subscribes to. Always check before paying for online content in case you can access it for free at a local library.

Search for your topic in the surprising number of pages in your library's "own" (through subscription fees) section of the invisible Web. Go to your library's list of its databases to find one relevant to your topic or look for a good general database.

Another way to find some of the invisible information on your topic is to look for directories to the deep pages of the Web. Use *Google* to search for *"invisible Web directories"* and click on a link there. You may not be able to type a search into invisible Web directories but you can move through a list of categories until you find one that covers your area. Once you find the appropriate area you will find a number of websites to use.

You can also perform a search in a conventional Web search engine using the term for your topic with the word database, for example, *crime database*. Suddenly you have links to research and sites such as the European and International Research Group on Crime, Ethics, and Social Philosophy (ERCES). This content-rich site may have remained forever unknown to the average searcher who has no knowledge of the invisible Web.

The Invisible College

More invisible information? Yes, and it may not rely directly on information technology. Direct communication among scientists and scholars has been part of the information cycle for a very long time. It was called by many the "invisible college" because it was not a formally organized system. These colleges were groups of people who were working in the same subject field and who communicated with each other through correspondence and telephone calls, all informal means of communication that were not recorded anywhere. Networking, as it is called today, includes all those earlier means—still in use—as well as e-mail and even the conversations that occur between colleagues at meetings.

Many students, scholars, and scientists now belong to electronic networks and social media sites that have services such as discussion groups, chat rooms, listservs, and bulletin boards that allow direct communication with colleagues around the world. No longer do researchers have to wait for the publication of reports in paper journals, a process that can take months or years, because much of that information is now published first or solely electronically.

The invisible college is informal and usually unpublished information, so that you as a researcher do not have access to it. But you may gain access through another person, for example, your professor, who may be a good resource to try whether or not they are connected to electronic networks because professors are almost certainly connected to the invisible network of direct communication among colleagues in their subject field.

Another access route to unpublished material is through search tools that include papers presented at conferences and academic meetings. These search tools include databases and directories, all segments of the invisible Web. So you will find some of the invisible college's resources by searching the invisible Web.

Once you feel comfortable with the various ways in which information is communicated you will be able to make quicker decisions about resources that really fill your information needs.

CONCEPT CHECK

Compare search results in a search engine such as *Yahoo!* with the results from a database your library subscribes to. What differences do you see in the types of resources?

TYPES OF EVALUATIVE CRITERIA

There are two main types of evaluative criteria. The first type is based on information characteristics, and the second type is based on the content of the information resources. The information characteristics covered in Chapter 1 are not context based but are intrinsic to the material. Look at the requirements of your assignment: does your professor require you to use at least one primary resource? Do you need objective or subjective information? Must all your resources be scholarly or can some be popular?

Careful evaluation to meet an information need requires you to be aware of several more information characteristics that are relative to your specific topic. For your topic:

- Do you need only current information, only historical information, or some of each?
- How technical or advanced must the information be? Are you required to use only "scholarly sources?"
- How much information do you need; i.e., how many resources are necessary?

Current or Historical?

It is important to pay attention to the date of the resources you use. Researchers who look for books on their topics without checking the publication dates can be in danger of using old information that has recently been disproved or drastically changed in some way. If you are looking for current resources, it is important to sort your search results by date because many databases display search results by relevance. Other assignments may require resources published within a certain amount of time, the last five years, for example. Sometimes a professor will remind you to use timely information. Timely information is a relative concept, meaning that the definition of the word timely can change from topic to topic. Examples of topics with different time-related needs are:

- *Influenza* (flu). With so many changes in this topic every year, the most current information may be needed almost exclusively so that the researcher can cover the virus's mutations, prevention, etc.
- *Immigration.* This issue is always current but also has a long history suitable for research. Including older resources on immigration in the U.S. might help clarify current opinions about it. A well-rounded research paper on such a topic would benefit from both historical and current information.
- *Strategies used in the U.S. Civil War.* Because this is obviously an historical topic you could write a very good report using older information.

The aspect of your topic that you select will influence whether you must search for very recent or historical information or both. Often topics seem to require only very recent information but that need will change depending on your focus. See Figure 3–1 for an example of two books—one older and one more recent—on the sample topic *influenza.*

The topic may be medical (influenza vaccination), scientific (genetic strains), or sociological (workforce impact), but many projects that deal with it would benefit from historical information as well as very current.

Just as topics may be covered in several subject fields, they may also be addressed using information from various time periods. Keep in mind that a book recently published can contain historical information. Basically you must look at the date of every resource you intend to use.

 SEARCH TIP

Topics can influence whether you need current or historical information, or both.

| **Figure 3–1** | A 1976 Book and a 2005 Book on the Topic of Influenza |

Imperato, P. J. (1976). *What to do about the flu.* New York: Dutton.
Kolata, G. B. (2005). *Flu: The story of the great influenza pandemic of 1918 and the search for the virus that caused it.* New York: Simon & Schuster.

Technical, Scholarly, or General?

One objective of a research assignment is to give you the chance to develop your knowledge, to incorporate new information into your knowledge base. This means you can suit the level of technicality to your own needs. Sometimes professors decide the technical/general question for you by requiring you to use specific resources or by outlawing others. When you have to make the decision yourself, consider the following criteria.

■   What level is the course for which you are doing the assignment?

The technical nature of information should be viewed as a continuum with very general information at one end and expert-level at the other. Where does your own level of knowledge fit and how much is it expected to grow? Think of where your course would fit in this range. Select materials appropriate to meet these conditions.

■   Does your professor require you to use scholarly sources only?

In-depth analysis is generally found in **scholarly** resources such as books or journal articles. Authors of scholarly resources almost always document their work by providing bibliographies that list the materials they consulted before writing. (Reminder: those bibliographies can expand your own research with minimum effort on your part because you can find the resources that are listed in the bibliographies without doing another search yourself.) **Popular** resources are those that are intended for use by the general public, such as magazines (*Time, People, Popular Science,* etc.) and newspapers.

A scholarly resource may also be called a refereed resource. A **refereed** resource is one in which information is published only after it has been reviewed by several experts in that subject field. It may also be called **peer reviewed.** The refereeing/reviewing process means that an author submits work to an editor who sends it to other experts in the field (peers) who then review the content carefully. For some resources this means that the experiment reported in the article is repeated by another expert; for other resources it means that materials in the bibliography are carefully checked; for most it means that the writing is checked for factual honesty and grammatical correctness. Many databases now include easy methods for selecting refereed/peer reviewed/scholarly records only. See Figure 3–2.

The differences between scholarly and popular resources often puzzle new researchers. Figure 3–3 outlines the major distinctions, which also apply to the differences between general resources and some technical information resources.

◆   **SEARCH TIP**

Check the database search screen for the option to limit your search to peer-reviewed articles. It can make your searching much easier!

Figure 3–2	Option to Select Scholarly Resources Only (in circle) on a Database's Search Form Web-page: www.il.proquest.com.

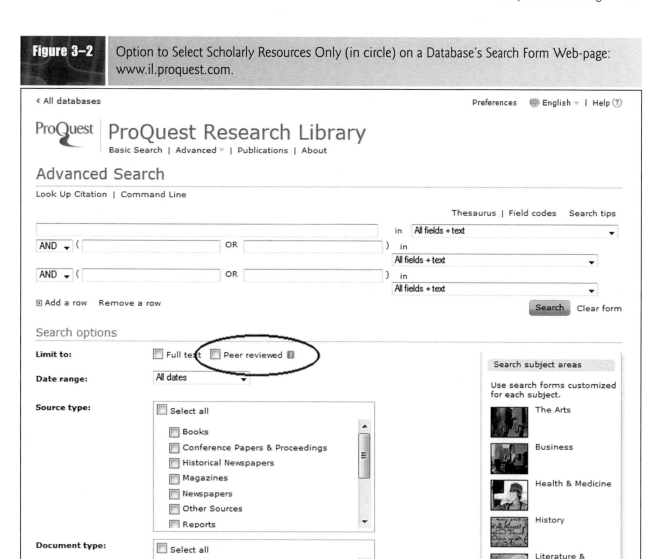

The images and their contents are published with permission of ProQuest LLC. Further reproduction is prohibited without permission.

Figure 3–3	General/Popular vs. Scholarly Information

General or popular information	Scholarly information
Intended for non-expert public	Intended for practitioners, researchers, or experts in the subject area
May have information that has not been reviewed by experts	Contains information that has been written and often reviewed by experts
Provides brief factual reporting that may be fleshed out with some analyses of factors involved	Provides information on latest research and scholarship
Useful when a researcher needs broad information on a topic	Useful when a researcher needs in-depth analysis of a topic
Found in magazines and other sources	Found in journals and other sources

| **Figure 3–4** | Results from Different Search Tools for the Same Topic |

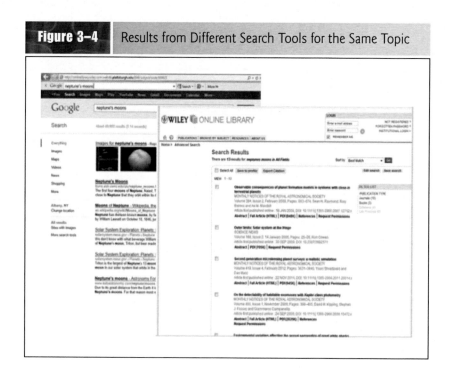

■ With whom will you share your understanding of the information you retrieve in your research?

Often your reader; i.e., your professor, already knows a great deal about your topic. If so, the information on which you base your paper can be more technical than that found in resources you use to provide information for a speech delivered in your Public Speaking 101 class. And if the research is for personal interest you will instinctively select materials that meet your level of knowledge or skill.

■ Are you able to understand immediately from the title of the resource what it will be about, or do you have to read through the title several times to decipher the subject of the article or book?

Select search tools that lead you to information resources that are at the desired level of technicality. Too general a search tool may result in materials that include only introductory information that both you and your audience will find boring, while at the other end of the spectrum your use of too narrowly focused search tools can bring you information too advanced for your use.

Where you look for resources is influenced by your decision regarding the technical level of information. See the examples in Figure 3–4. A search on the topic of Neptune's moons was performed in two different search tools. *Google* is on the left. The right example is from the *Wiley Online Library,* a database that covers scientific resources.

You can glimpse items on the continuum from popular to technical in Figure 3-4 from the different tools. Researchers with very advanced knowledge of astronomy would be comfortable using a detailed NASA database. Would you? You can see why it is smart to pay attention to the tool(s) you use.

Figure 3–5	Types of Publications Available through Various Databases

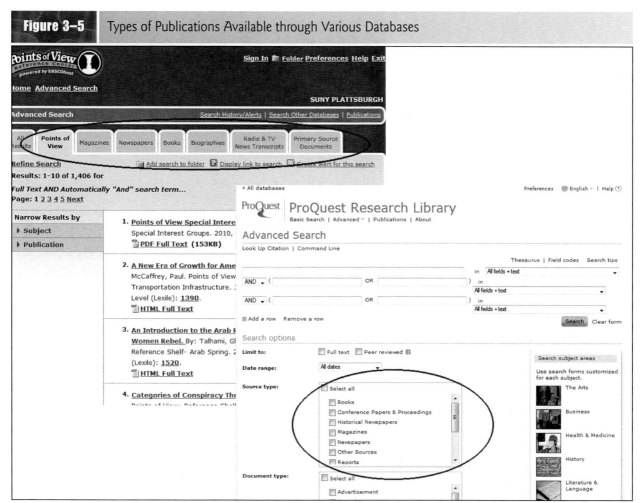

The images and their contents are published with permission of ProQuest LLC. Further reproduction is prohibited without permission. Web-page: www.il.proquest.com.

Selecting the Type of Publication(s)

This is a choice that is new to some researchers. Many databases now include many types of publications, not just periodicals. When your professor states that you must include in your bibliography "newspaper accounts from the time" or "analyses from relevant trade magazines" how do you know what's what? For example, what is a trade magazine? How do you find what you need? Databases usually offer you the option of selecting the type(s) you want to use from a drop-down menu or an index of publication types. Some use tabbed menus that many researchers overlook. See Figure 3–5.

In one of the databases in Figure 3–5 you can select journal articles as a publication type. Be sure you look at what is available from a database and if you are not sure what is meant by some of the choices, look it up in the database's Help screens or ask your librarian. You may find exactly what you need when you know what your choices are AND you read the screen.

HOW MANY RESOURCES?

Many professors give students a specific number of resources they must consult before writing their research papers. Librarians at reference desks hear students asking for help to find "just one more thing because I have to have seven," or earlier in the students' research, for help finding "one place where I can find five scholarly resources on (your topic here)." The length of the final product—speech, paper, or group presentation—should provide guidance on how many resources are needed.

Use enough information resources to understand your topic. While you often want to be told a precise number of how many resources you must use, you should keep in mind the final goal of the research project: your professor wants you to understand your topic well enough to report your understanding coherently and completely, to synthesize new information with what you already knew and are learning in their course. As you progress in your own research and writing skills, you will develop a sense of when you have enough information. Do not forget, however, that you must follow the dictates of the assignment if your professor does specify a particular number of resources.

After you have considered all the above components in the information research process, it is time to move to the next step.

Locate and Retrieve Relevant Information Resources

Use Technological Tools for Accessing Information

This step in the process is what most people think of as information research. It is the actual activity of looking up a topic to get information. The mechanics of the search make up this first stage of the research process. Chapter 2 took you through the actions involved.

Retrieve Information Resources

Not all publications indexed by a database are available in full text in that database. If your assignment's deadline is coming up fast, you may need only full text materials. You learned earlier that many full text databases are not completely full text, but most allow you to limit your search so that only full text items are retrieved. When you find your perfect resource, say, a periodical article, in a database that does not have it in full text, does your library provide a mechanism for you to discover if it might be available full text in any other? Services called link resolvers, such as *Ex Libris SFX* and EBSCO's *A to Z,* may be available to you. They enable you to look for the title of your periodical to see if you can get the article full text online in *any* of your library's databases. These are just two examples of services that search for periodicals. Another phenomenon that is growing rapidly online is called Open Access Journals. Journals that are available full text online without (sometimes very costly) subscriptions are called open access. Anyone can use articles from these journals even if they or their libraries do not subscribe to them—in print or online. You can try searching for such periodicals; use *Google*'s *Directory* under *open access journals,* for example. Many libraries provide links to directories of open access journals. See Figure 3–6 for an example of this.

As you can see, the library provides several ways to help you determine if a periodical you need is available somewhere in full text.

Interlibrary Loan: If your perfect resource is not a periodical article but rather is a chapter in a book, it may be more difficult to find it online because most books are still NOT yet digitized

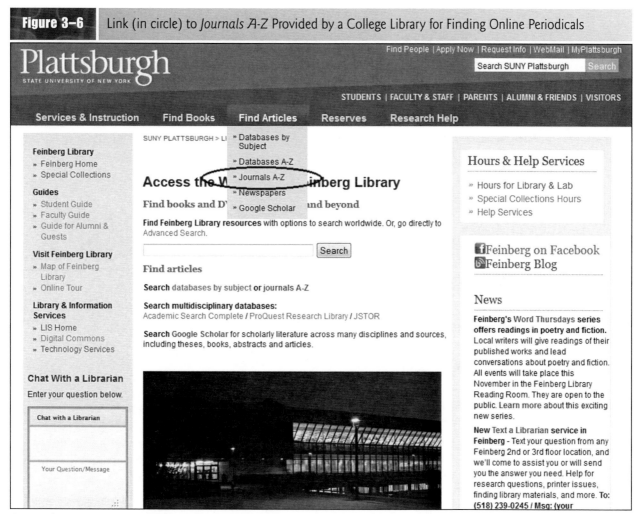

Figure 3-6 | Link (in circle) to *Journals A-Z* Provided by a College Library for Finding Online Periodicals

Copyright © SUNY Plattsburgh. Reprinted by permission.

(contrary to the hope and belief of many students.). There is another library service that is part of the retrieval process: interlibrary loan or I.L.L. This service allows a researcher in any location to get an information resource from almost any other location in the world. You do this by requesting an information item from another library through the InterLibrary Loan department in your library. You can often place the request using a link to the service inside the database you are searching, making the process simple and easy. Look for language such as "Get this item now" or "Find a copy." The I.L.L. staff complete the transaction, sending out the request for the item and notifying

SKILL CHECK

Locate databases relevant to your academic major. List three that you might use to find sources for a research project.

you when it is received. Some I.L.L. departments deliver the materials directly to you by email or home delivery if you are an online learner.

In many places the greatest investment the researcher must make to use this service is TIME, because even with electronic exchange of materials the staff needs time to check your request for accuracy and send it on to the lending library. The lending library still needs time to locate and deliver your request. Delivery times for I.L.L. keep getting faster and faster, so it is important to check out this worthwhile service at your library.

The criteria and techniques above are all parts of the research process. The next step named in this chapter may well be the most important.

Evaluate Information Resources

This step is gaining in importance with every advance in information technology. The more information retrieved easily, the more difficult it may be to find the best to fill your information needs. You may find evaluation to be the step you repeat most often as you look over the many references retrieved in every search you do.

Evaluate Evaluate Evaluate Evaluate

The heading for this section is meant to be heard as an ever-repeating echo because it should be done constantly during your research. The evaluation process, an integral part of the whole research process, is crucial to retrieving meaningful facts, data, opinions, and analyses of your research topic.

The dictionary definition of evaluate is: "to determine the significance, worth, or condition of usually by *careful appraisal* and study" (Merriam Webster Online Dictionary, authors' *underline* for emphasis http://www.merriam-webster.com/dictionary/evaluate).

You evaluate without realizing it in many aspects of your life, not just while you are doing research. The flexibility that is characteristic of a good research process assumes that you are evaluating information resources as you go along, keeping and discarding items based on your criteria. For example, these are all evaluative questions:

- Whose pizza is best?
- Is that pair of boots worth its price?
- Which professor has the best reputation for teaching a particular course?
- Should you buy regular or special or premium gasoline for your car?
- Which of the 4,090,000 Web pages on *Iroquois* found by *Google* are worth pursuing?

When evaluating information, the type of media that carries the information can influence its value; e.g., you might hear that you must evaluate information you get from the Web while little or nothing is said about judging books or periodical articles. But **ALL information resources need to be *selected* by you because computers do not make evaluative decisions, YOU do.**

How do you go about evaluating, using careful appraisal, and get your assignment in on time? Give yourself a measuring stick: set up some criteria.

Evaluative Criteria

Criteria are the characteristics you use as measuring sticks. The word criteria is used often in college discussions and assignments because it is useful in so many settings. Examples of evaluative criteria vary widely, from concrete objects such as weight standards; e.g., one criterion for a professional bantamweight boxer is that he can weigh no more than 119 lbs., to abstract concepts; e.g., the criteria needed to make a statement a syllogism are a major premise, a minor premise, and a conclusion. Criteria for evaluating information tools and resources while you do your research are:

- Author
- Title
- Date of publication
- Publisher

These criteria are good for evaluating resources *during* your search. Once you have the resources in hand you should use criteria that help you measure the content of the materials. A closer look at the first glance criterion starts this discussion of evaluation standards.

Author

As stated earlier, looking at the author of an information resource can be a very quick way to evaluate the resource. Are you familiar with the name? Did the author write the textbook for your class? Or if the name is unfamiliar, does it appear as an author throughout the references retrieved on your topic? Answering yes to any of those questions means you can consider your resource *authoritative,* written by someone with a good understanding of the topic. Some databases include "Author Affiliation" in their citations and this can give you the helpful information that your author is affiliated with a particular university or college, which may indicate authority in a subject field.

Is there an author named? This may or may not be important to you. Popular magazines rely on staff members to write articles; frequently there is no author named with the article, no byline beneath the title. Scholarly resources include authors' names. Do all your resources have to be scholarly?

Web pages may present difficulties to researchers looking for the pages' authors. The pages may be on websites similar to magazines, with unnamed authors responsible for the pages. Or the pages may be part of someone's personal website, and you learn this by going to the end of the page and finding a "Contact me" link or a link to the larger site. Does this fit into the requirements of your assignment in particular, and the trustworthiness of the information in general?

If this criterion cannot be met; i.e., if you cannot find an author's name or you are uncertain about their authority on the topic, will you still be able to use the resource? Perhaps the resource can prove its worth through the other criteria.

Title

Select resources whose titles you can understand immediately. Look for familiar terms for your topic in the title. The exact words you used as search terms do not have to be part of the title, but words in the title that you know are closely related to your topic make your decisions easier.

Webpage titles can be very quick clues about their usefulness, along with the pages' first line of text that are provided by a Web search engine. See the examples in Figure 3–7.

 SEARCH TIP

Criteria such as author, title, and date can be used while searching; other criteria such as reliability, coverage, and scope are better used when you have retrieved the resource.

A student researching the topic *customs of indigenous peoples* should be able to choose from those listed in Figure 3–7 a website that would be likely to satisfy the "scholarly resource" requirements of her assignment. Of course, looking through the entire site will be the surest way to determine whether it meets the criterion.

Date of Publication

The importance of this information is discussed earlier in this chapter. When was the book published, or what's the date of the journal or magazine or newspaper? If the references retrieved in a database are all dated 1986 or earlier, is that workable for your topic and assignment? Check to see what dates that database covers.

Can you find a date on a Web site you're considering? Is it a copyright date or does it say "Latest revision" and give the date? If their is no way to determine the date of the information, use that resource with caution. There are surprisingly many pages that were put on the Web that have never been updated. This may be one of the reasons that some professors ban all websites as resources for student assignments.

Publisher

In the days of paper-only resources this criterion meant little to undergraduate students new to literature research. Graduate level research is more advanced and researchers become familiar with publishers in their fields. Publishers of print resources will become more easily recognizable as you progress in your own college research. This criterion is far more important when reviewing a webpage.

One type of publisher on the Web may be indicated by the Top Domain Level (TDL) in a URL. There is a limited number of TDLs in use—that number is expanding—and they can indicate, only *broadly,* what type of institution or agency or business is supporting the Web site, where its server is. Possible indicators of reliability include *.edu, .gov, .mil,* and to a lesser extent, *.org.* These TDLs tell you that the server is provided by a college or university, a government agency, a military branch, or an organization (such as the Red Cross Red Crescent at www.ifrc.org), respectively. Just remember that this is a fairly crude evaluation tool.

The Web has made knowing the publisher important for all researchers, new and experienced. A Web page may be authored by a person and published in a corporate site, or may be self-published, as are a great number of Web pages. (The word corporate here refers to any entity of more than one person; e.g., an organization or corporation hosting or sponsoring a Web site.) An individual may publish himself whatever he wishes by using a free Web host; a page that includes *.geocities* or *.aol,* for example, as part of its URL is most likely a self-published page created by someone who uses the Web host GeoCities or AOL. The stature of the person—or corporate entity—responsible for putting a page or site on the Web will help you decide whether to use the information it contains. The two Web pages below illustrate this point. Both were retrieved in a *Google* search under *"capital punishment" juveniles.* Figure 3–8a is from an individual's site and Figure 3–8b is from the American Bar Association's site. A researcher should scroll to the bottom of the "CAPITAL PUNISHMENT:" article to get more information about the site, whereas no further research into the publisher of the ABA page is necessary. See also the comments above under Author.

The above standards helped you decide which items you want to retrieve in their entirety. Now your task is to begin evaluating these materials based on their content.

 SEARCH TIP

Go to the end of a webpage to look for the date of publication.

Figure 3-7	Titles of Web Pages Retrieved by a Search Engine with Brief Excerpts from the Pages

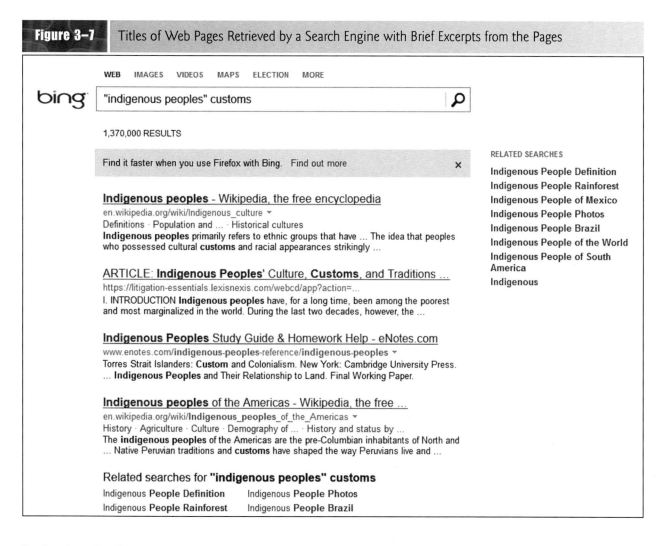

Evaluating the Content of Resources for the Integration Phase of the Research Process

Once you have information resources in hand, such as books or periodical articles you have retrieved from the library, and periodical articles and Web pages you have on-screen, you have to look at their content. *Read* what you have found. Then ask yourself again whether the resources meet the information requirements that are set out early in this chapter. Is the resource too dated to be useful? Is it too technical? Do you have enough information to complete the research project? The criteria you might use in judging the content of resources include:

- Scope or coverage
- Writing style
- Objectivity
- Documentation
- Reviews

Examine each criterion more closely to see whether you will need it to help make your selections.

Scope or Coverage

Does the resource cover the whole subject into which your topic falls, or just the aspect you have chosen, or perhaps only part of that aspect? How does it fill in your knowledge of your topic? A

Figure 3–8a A Web Page "Published" by an Individual <http://www.aztlan.net/acuna5.htm>

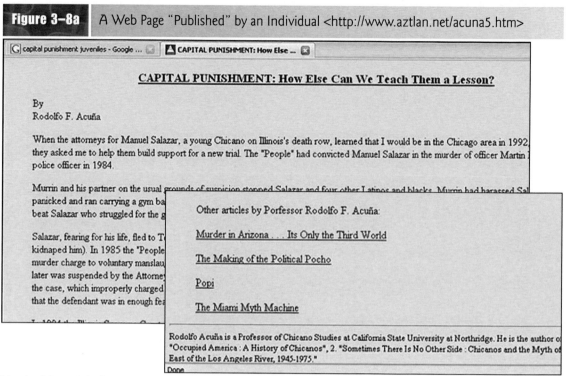

Used with permission.

Figure 3–8b A Web Page Published by a Corporate Entity

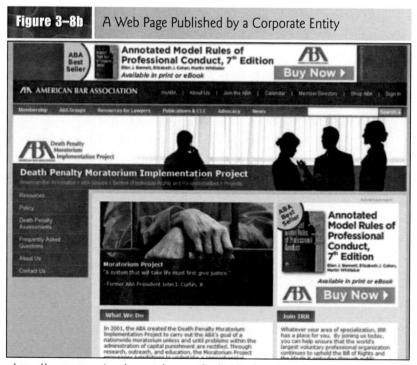

<http://www.americanbar.org/groups/individual_rights/projects/death_penaltyoratorium_implementation_project.html>. "ABA Website Screenshot" 2012.

broad resource such as a book may include a good section or chapter that addresses your aspect thoroughly. Use the book's table of contents or index as your guide. Periodical articles, on the other hand, are narrowly focused, usually covering only one aspect of the subject. If that aspect is the one you have selected as your topic, the resource should be very valuable. You discover a resource's worth by reading it through. If a resource turns out not to be what you want you should not hesitate to look for a better one, using what you learned from any rejected source to revise your search.

Writing Style

Is the material in your resource well written? It may be written too simply for your level of knowledge, or it may be a resource that overwhelms you with details about the topic that are not necessary for your approach. This criterion is closely related to the general/technical question posed earlier. It also speaks to the differences between scholarly and popular resources. The writing style should be slightly above your own level but not so technical or abstruse that you cannot understand it.

Objectivity

Objectivity may or may not be required of all your resources. And it can be difficult to determine whether a resource is presenting its information in an unbiased manner. Bias is ubiquitous, that is, it is everywhere. And it, like beauty, may be arguably in the eye of the beholder. For example, many would say that the organization Greenpeace is a good environmental organization. But others object to its tactics and consider it bad. The value of information from the Greenpeace Web site can vary significantly depending upon its use. It could contribute valuable information to a paper on activists and their strategies; conversely, it may be considered detrimental to use statistics from the Greenpeace site because of the group's pro-environment bias. The wars in Iraq and Afghanistan have brought up news stories about the bias in news reporting in the United States, news coverage being a resource whose objectivity has been taken for granted for some time. Is the news objective? Clearly this is a criterion that you will have to judge for yourself.

Look for loaded words in the resource. For example, a person who opposes or disbelieves an idea or opinion may describe it as dangerous. Similarly, someone in favor of a concept or belief may use very positive words to portray it, such as undeniable reasons. Unfortunately, not all biased resources are so blatant in showing their slant. You may only be aware of a tone in the text or an attitude in a video resource that indicates support of an idea or opposition to it. Many times you must be quite familiar with the topic and its internal controversies in order to spot a resource that supports only one side or the other. The best help in deciding about whether to use a particular resource because of—or in spite of—its bias may come from a subject expert such as your professor.

CONCEPT CHECK

The Web is not the only place that subjective, information is found. Look carefully at the objectivity of ALL your information resources. Select two publications you often see or use, and rate their objectivity using the chart in Figure 3–9.

Figure 3–9	Indicators of Scholarship and Propaganda

How to tell the difference between scholarly work and propaganda	
Indicators of scholarship	*Indicators of propaganda*
Describes limits of research or data	*Excessive claims of certainty; i.e., one "right" way*
Presents accurate description of alternate viewpoints	*Relies on personal attacks and ridicule*
Encourages debate, discussion, and criticism	*Emotional appeals and use of inflammatory language*
Settles disputes by use of generally accepted criteria for evaluating data	*Suppresses contradictory views*
Looks for counter-examples	*Appeals to popular prejudices*
Updates information	*Devalues critical appraisal*
Admits own ignorance	*Transforms words and statistics to suit purpose*
Relies on critical thinking skills	*Presents information and views out of context*

Source http://ilstu.libguides.com/

Documentation

This criterion also relates to the scholarly or popular quality of a resource. An article—or chapter or book or webpage—that has a bibliography provides you with evidence that the writer found information resources that support the information you are reading. Scholarly resources almost always have documentation of the resources their authors used, listed in a bibliography or list of references. Popular resources are far less likely to list the sources used.

This attribute of an information resource can help determine its slant—or lack thereof. A list of resources used may reveal if the author consulted information that presented both sides of a controversial topic. Look closely at the bibliographies included with *Wikipedia* articles, for example. The fact that anyone can contribute information to the *Wikipedia* should cause you to consider all its information very carefully. Regardless of the slant of a resource, however, when selecting resources for a college-level research project, those with bibliographies are almost always preferable to those without.

Reviews

Not all resources have or need reviews for support. If you are uncertain of the bias of the resource, such as a book or video about your topic, look for reviews. There are standard tools for finding reviews and your librarian can help you use the reviewing tools your library subscribes to.

PULLING THE EVALUATIVE CRITERIA TOGETHER WITH STAR

This chapter has introduced many evaluative criteria for the multiple phases of research. Whatever criteria you apply will have a significant impact on your research projects. It might be difficult for you to remember all the criteria once you start your research, especially if you are also trying to

 SEARCH TIP

Does the resource you are looking at have a lengthy bibliography? If so, it is most likely a scholarly resource.

learn about a new topic. It might be tempting to just forget about all this and use the first ten resources that you located.

One way to more easily remember to evaluate is by the mnemonic acronym STAR. You might have learned the mnemonic HOMES in grade school to help you remember all the Great Lakes (Huron, Ontario, Michigan, Erie, and Superior). Mnemonics work well because it is easier to remember a short word or phrase than it is to remember a long list. The phrase then jogs your memory enough to remember the list items.

STAR: USING ALL THE CRITERIA TO MAKE YOUR FINAL SELECTIONS

The STAR criteria pull together all the different planning, searching, and integrating criteria into one simple set. It is important to learn the criteria separately so that you really understand them, and then for greater efficiency after learning them individually, you can apply them in groups. Think of now selecting resources that have star qualities and you'll remember to evaluate with ***STAR: Scholarship, Timeliness, Authority, and Relevance.*** See Figure 3–10 for the STAR criteria.

Figure 3–10	STAR Criteria for Evaluating Sources

Scholarship: Evidence of careful investigation of fact and analysis of opinion.
Questions to ask: Is the information accurate when checked against other sources? Is the writing style popular, technical, or academic in tone and language? Is this new information or a summarization of older information? How reliable and error-free is the information? Is there evidence of potential bias? Does the author have a specific agenda or point-of-view? Does the author explain where the information was obtained? Does the information include a bibliography or list of sources used?

Timeliness: Currency of the publication and of its bibliography.
Questions to ask: Is the publication date clearly stated? When was the book last published or the web page last revised? Is it maintained and updated regularly? Are any links on the web page up-to-date and useable? Is the information current or historical enough for your topic? How do the publication dates in the bibliography or list of sources compare to the publication date of the information resource?

Authority: Expertise, knowledge, and experience.
Questions to ask: Is it clear who is authoring, sponsoring, or publishing the information? Is the sponsor or publisher legitimate? Is it clear who wrote the information? Are the qualifications (educational degrees, job experience, eyewitness status) of the author clearly stated? How does the author know about this topic? Is the author affiliated with an institution or organization? Is that institution connected to the topic? Is there contact information available for the author of the document?

Relevance: Direct focus on the topic or research question.
Questions to ask: Does the information cover the subject adequately? Are there inexplicable omissions? What is the purpose of the information: i.e., to inform, convince, or sell? What does it contribute to the literature in the field? Who is the intended audience based on content, tone, and style? What is the overall value of the content compared to the range of resources on the topic?

H. Heller-Ross, 2008. Modified and adapted with permission from *Evaluating Internet Resources: Points to Consider* (2002) Milner Library, Illinois State University. http://www.mlb.ilstu.edu/ressubj/subject/intrnt/evaluate.htm

Bottom Line: Be Selective!

Set standards for your resources. Use criteria to help you select good resources to pursue. Use criteria to decide how good those resources are once you have them in hand. Be selective while you are doing research. It will keep you from working more than necessary to make sense out of hastily selected resources when you write your paper.

Now that you have the information, you must complete your assignment and *use* the information.

CHAPTER HIGHLIGHTS

- ■ To determine the information requirements of your assignment you must consider your intended audience. The requirements include questions of:
  - ● Current or historical information.
  - ● Technical or general information.
  - ● Number of resources.

- ■ Locating and retrieving information resources involves using appropriate information technologies including catalogs, databases, and the Web, and sometimes your library's Interlibrary Loan service.

- ■ Evaluate the possible value of information resources on a first-glance basis *while* you do your research, using the following criteria:
  - ● Author: must each resource have a named author?
  - ● Title: can you readily understand a resource's title? If yes, you're likely to be able to understand the information that resource provides.
  - ● Date of Publication: is there a timeliness criterion that is part of your information requirements?
  - ● Publisher: will the top domain level in a web page's URL be helpful as a first-scan clue to reliable information for this assignment?

- ■ Evaluate the content of information resources when you have them *in hand* or on-screen. Use the criteria above as well as:
  - ● Scope or coverage.
  - ● Writing style.
  - ● Objectivity.
  - ● Documentation.
  - ● Reviews.

- ■ You should evaluate information resources retrieved in a search by using the clues contained in the references in search tools before you print anything or get any books from the stacks.

- ■ Clues in search tools' entries include words or phrases in the title (and subtitle) of an article or book, and an author's name appearing often in one or more tools.

- ■ The periodical databases to which your library subscribes are part of the invisible Web, as are e-books and back issues of many newspapers.

- ■ The information hidden in the invisible Web is accessible to searchers through databases and online directories.

- ■ The invisible college consists of unpublished communication among researchers: phone calls, e-mail, unpublished papers presented at conferences, even conversations at those conferences. A student researcher may have access to this information by talking to her professor or searching for databases that include references to unpublished materials or those waiting to be published.

CHAPTER 3

Questions

1. A student wants to give an informative speech in their Public Speaking class (COM 101) on the public's fascination with the idea of space travel and the developing aeronautical innovations to make it more accessible. Does a topic such as this require any historical documentation? Explain your answer.

2. Select a database to which your library subscribes that you would recommend to the student in Question 1. What types of resources will she retrieve from it? Why are you recommending this database?

3. The student is Question 1 is required to turn in a bibliography for the speech. How many resources would you advise them to use to support their final ten-minute speech? Explain your answer.

Integrating

While you are enrolled in college, you have access to unprecedented amounts of information through your libraries' websites, including online books, articles from journals, magazines, newspapers, streaming media, maps, rare books, and manuscripts, to name a few. The databases to which your library subscribes, tools such as *JSTOR, ScienceDirect, ProQuest,* and *EBSCO,* allow you access to information that you would not have had otherwise or would have to a more limited extent through your public library. These search tools are not freely available on the Web; content of these databases is licensed and restricted. While these databases are ubiquitous on North American college campuses, they are unaffordable in much of the rest of the non-western world. The scholars who write the articles that get published in these databases, too, are primarily from the western world.

The Open Access (OA) movement advocates the free dissemination and exchange of peer-reviewed scholarly and scientific information without copyright or licensing restrictions. According to the Budapest Open Access Initiative (2002), "The only constraint on reproduction and distribution, and the only role for copyright in this domain, should be to give authors control over the integrity of their work and the right to be properly acknowledged and cited." Students, too, can actively engage in the OA movements through a variety of efforts, including participating in the Sparky Awards (<http://www.sparkyawards.org/>).

How are your life and the lives of others impacted by the creation, dissemination, and access to information? Beacons of an Information Society, The Alexandria Proclamation on Information Literacy and Lifelong Learning (International Federation of Library Associations and Institutions, 2005), states:

> Information Literacy lies at the core of lifelong learning. It empowers people in all walks of life to seek, evaluate, use and create information effectively to achieve their personal, social, occupational and educational goals. It is a basic human right in a digital world and promotes social inclusion of all nations.

Information literacy incorporates more than just information research techniques and the use of technology. An information literate world citizen can define their information need, find the information to address the need using appropriate tools and technologies, and add the retrieved information into their body of knowledge. Those elements of information literacy have been addressed in the earlier chapters of this book. An information literate citizen is also aware of information and information technology (IT) in the broadest context, as components of the social and political life of the world.

ETHICAL, LEGAL, AND SOCIOECONOMIC ISSUES SURROUNDING INFORMATION AND INFORMATION TECHNOLOGY

Fast-moving changes in information technology create concerns and challenges. Issues that are becoming more obvious to you as a researcher and IT user are the social and ethical implications of available information and IT: questions of bias, censorship and filtering, privacy rights, ownership, plagiarism, and information haves and have-nots.

As information technology makes storing, retrieving, and producing information easier and easier, it creates challenges.

First, we will focus on plagiarism, from un-documented insertion of phrases and sentences to buying or trading complete research papers from the Web. That will introduce several other broad concepts, moving from those that affect you personally to concerns with a global reach: 1) ownership of information, including questions of copyright and downloading and peer-to-peer (P2P) file sharing; 2) privacy rights, concentrating on the ownership of personal or private information and the ethical use of information in various contexts; 3) bias and censorship, focusing on protection versus free access to information; and 4) the digital divide, introducing the socioeconomic paradox of burgeoning information technology, a paradox because "more is better" can be a less-than-good thing. This discussion will serve as a preface to your exploration of these concepts throughout your college career. Questions will surface that will require your thought and attention throughout your life.

CITATION vs. PLAGIARISM

Once you have included the resources you discovered during the research process for your project, you must cite your sources. As you begin your research, you can begin managing your references and research immediately; you do not need to wait until the end of your paper or project to begin the process. Software known as bibliographic management software can help to organize and create citations. Commonly known programs include *EndNote, Zotero, Mendeley,* and *RefWorks*. Regardless of how or when you choose to manage your research, if you do not properly attribute the ideas, the paraphrasing, and the direct quotes that you relied on, you may inadvertently plagiarize. A general rule is, if you use it, cite it!

CONCEPT CHECK

Lifelong learning is a basic human right in the digital world. What are some other basic human rights in the digital world and how do those compare with lifelong learning? List two reasons why you agree or disagree.

You have completed the research process of your assignment; that is a significant accomplishment but much hard work still remains. You have scoured through bibliographies and databases and have read many articles, book chapters, and other content. You have reflected on what you have learned and how that information informs your paper or project. Are there any gaps in your research? Do you need to go back and search again? Research is an iterative process and it is time-consuming, but it is satisfying and worthwhile. Once you have determined that your research is complete and you have compiled all your resources, you have to cite your sources following the style guide required by your professor or preferred by your major or academic discipline.

Whether or not your professor required that you cite your sources at the end of your research paper, you must do so.

Reasons to Cite Sources

The most important reason that you cite your sources is to give credit where credit is due: to acknowledge the other creators and authors of the information which you have used and from whom you have learned. Even when you do not use direct quotes, you need to report the sources you used because you took the ideas from those sources and integrated them with your own. You inform your audience that those creators helped you learn what you just incorporated in your paper. If you paraphrase it, cite it.

If you do not cite the sources on which your work is based you are guilty of stealing someone else's ideas; you are guilty of plagiarism. To plagiarize is "to steal and use (the ideas or writings of another) as one's own," according to the *American Heritage Dictionary* (2000). Plagiarism is intellectual theft because you imply, through your lack of documentation, that all the ideas you present in your research paper or report or speech are yours and yours alone, that they sprang full-grown from your mind with no help from anyone else, when in reality they were shaped or came from others. Plagiarism is a falsification that is punished in most college courses by a failing grade, in many colleges and universities by severe penalties including dismissal from the school, in professional circles by ostracism from one's circle of colleagues and occasionally through civil lawsuits. Plagiarism is easily avoided: cite your sources.

Scholars list "References" or "Works Cited" in order to document their research. Academic work includes citation of sources so that researchers in that subject field can develop a picture of the research done by an author, how their thinking was shaped because of the work of others. When one is familiar with a subject field the bibliography helps illustrate the thought process of a writer. In many fields—especially in the Sciences—research is incremental; i.e., it builds upon earlier research. Documentation allows a researcher to find the exact source cited and use its information, its methods and theory, rather than creating their own through costly, time-consuming, and unnecessarily repetitive experiments.

Paraphrase or Quote?

You often paraphrase from resources you used: cite when you paraphrase. You are aware of the fact that a direct quote from a resource needs to be cited in your paper. What if you do not quote exactly? **Translating the thought of a sentence or paragraph from an information resource into your own words is *paraphrasing*.** When you encounter a new idea it is common for you to reword

 SEARCH TIP

The use of screenshots from the Web, tables, graphs, charts, and graphics *all* require citations in your papers.

it so that you understand and remember it. If you incorporate an idea or inspiration you gained from watching a video, from *YouTube* or from television, you must cite it. While it may seem awkward to work with in-text citations for paraphrasing, it is simply a matter of practice. An example of this is the following sentences from the *Encyclopedia Britannica Online* (2012):

> The baryons and mesons are complex subatomic particles built from more elementary objects, the quarks. Six types of quark, together with their corresponding antiquarks, are necessary to account for all the known hadrons. The six varieties, or "flavours," of quark have acquired the names up, down, charm, strange, top, and bottom.

If you used this as it is worded your professor would realize immediately it was from a published resource. This is because you have a writing voice that is not as academic as this paragraph sounds. Students sometimes assume that a professor will not notice a change in voice such as this. But think about how many student papers your professors have read, how familiar they are with student writing styles. They will spot it immediately. You would do better to use your own words. For example, your translation (paraphrase) of the *Britannica* paragraph might read more like this:

> Quarks are particles that are more elemental than subatomic particles. Quarks are named up quarks, down quarks, charmed quarks, strange, top, and bottom quarks. Baryons and mesons are built from quarks. Quarks and anti-quarks make up hadrons.

To get good advice and practice at paraphrasing use your college's writing help center, or go to established and respected websites such as OWL *(Purdue Online Writing Lab)*. See Figure 4–1.

When you paraphrase or quote anything, the best—and safest—approach is to **cite it if you use it.** Learning good citation habits as a college student begins a valuable lifelong behavior.

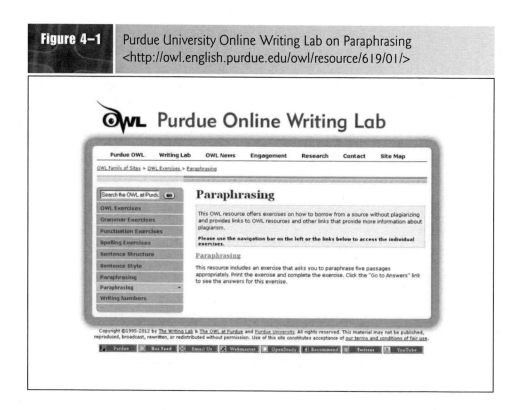

Figure 4–1 Purdue University Online Writing Lab on Paraphrasing
<http://owl.english.purdue.edu/owl/resource/619/01/>

Buying Papers Online aka Paper Mills

Self-service photocopy was an early reason that the general public became aware of copyright laws. When you pay for a photocopy of an article you are more easily aware that the information is not free for the taking. Cutting and pasting information from the Web may seem quite different because it appears to be waiting for you to use it . . . as yours and for free. Remember that **information on the Web is like any other information: if you quote it—or paraphrase it or cut-and-paste it—you *must* cite it.**

Completely written student papers can be purchased or obtained from some websites by agreeing to submit to the site a paper of your own in exchange. These sites are known as paper mills. You may have read articles about them in newspapers and magazines or heard them discussed on news programs or among your friends. The stories often arise because students have purchased papers and turned them in as their own; their deceptions were discovered and they were subjected to their institutions' penalties for plagiarism. Sites include *School Sucks* and *eCheat.com*. A paper mill's home page may have a disclaimer similar to the one in Figure 4–2 from *Papers123.com*. The size of the print is that found on the page.

Your professors are keenly aware of the paper-mill situation and are becoming more vigilant about the originality of information in your papers. They search the Web for plagiarized information and are talking to librarians, expert Web searchers who try to stay abreast of anti-plagiarism developments. There are software programs such as Turnitin.com to help faculty combat the problem. Now that you know how to do research so efficiently, do your own paraphrasing, quoting, writing, and citing, and proudly show off your own work.

THE MAKE-UP OF CITATIONS

The elements in any citation are the same but they are arranged differently depending on the style used. In addition to giving credit where credit is due, **the goal of every citation is to allow its reader or viewer to find the sources used.** Citations therefore must include enough information

Figure 4–2	Disclaimer from a Website That Makes Student Papers Available for Download

The intended purpose of our example college papers is that they be used as study aids or as models of what a good college paper should look like. We encourage students to use our reports to help them in quickening their research. Pursuant to New Jersey Statutes 2A:170–17.16–18 and similar statutes that exist in other states, The Paper Store Enterprises, Inc. will NEVER offer its services to ANY person giving ANY reason to believe that he or she intends to either wholly or partially submit our work for academic credit in their own name . . . Plagiarism is a CRIME! The Paper Store does not engage nor participate in any transactions for the purpose of assisting students in committing academic fraud. This service is NOT available to anyone who does not have a valid, ethical reason for seeking our assistance. The organization's rights to research, write, and globally-publish example college papers on the Internet are protected, Free Speech and shall continue unabated and uncensored.

CONCEPT CHECK

How does the availability of pre-written papers affect your life? Do you think that the dynamics in your classroom, such as the expectation of a level playing field among peers or faculty-student trust are impacted?

to accomplish this. **The elements of citations are universal: author(s), title, publication information.** The arrangement of these elements will differ somewhat depending on the citation format used and the item you cite: a book citation is slightly different from a video or website citation.

When you are using search tools, the elements of the citations shown in the results list are the elements you need to create a citation but they are not in a proper citation style that is usable for your research project. Check carefully the search tool you are using and look for the icon that indicates "Cite It" or "Export." Most academic search tools and databases have integrated citation managers to help you automatically generate a properly formatted citation according to many of the standard citation styles such as *MLA, APA, Chicago,* and *CSE.*

STYLE MANUALS AND FORMATS

Formats are precise and consistent standards for the arrangements of elements in citations. Various professional organizations and firms have created standards that are widely accepted in academic and professional circles. They are made available to researchers through numerous style manuals. Some professional organizations that have produced style manuals include the Modern Language Association (MLA), used by many subject fields in the Humanities (and in most high school classes); the American Psychological Association (APA), used by many departments in the Social Sciences; and the Council of Science Editors (CSE) and the American Chemical Society (ACS), used by many in the Sciences. The style usually followed by historians is the *Chicago Manual of Style.* An example of a manual created by a corporation is *The New York Times Style Manual.* Each of the style manuals provides guidelines for citation format and serves as a style guide for the layout of articles, research reports, and theses. The style manuals also include guidance for research and writing. The different style manuals are available in most libraries; there are many websites—often provided by libraries—that will help you create citations that follow these formats. As noted previously, one of the best examples of such a site is OWL, the *Purdue Online Writing Lab* <http://owl.english.purdue.edu/>.

If your professor specifies no particular citation format, choose a standard format and then be consistent. Elements in a citation always appear in a certain order in citations so that the user of a bibliography can easily recognize what's what in the citations and can easily locate the exact sources cited there. This means that you, as the creator of the bibliography, have to maintain the consistency established by the style manual's guidelines. Regardless of the style you are using, your journal sources must include the title of the periodical, its volume, issue, and date, and the page number(s) of the article.

Some examples of citations, similar to those that you would include in a reference list for a paper or research report, are given in Figure 4–3. The first citation illustrates how to cite a book, the second citation illustrates how to cite a journal article and the third illustrates how to cite a posting from the Web.

Figure 4–3	Example of References from a Student's Paper on the Zombie Phenomenon in Popular American Culture

Bishop, K. W. (2010). *American zombie gothic: The rise and fall (and rise) of the walking dead in popular culture.* Jefferson, NC: McFarland.

Newbury, M. (2012). Fast zombie/slow zombie: Food writing, horror movies, and agribusiness apocalypse. *American Literary History, 24*(1), 87–114.

Slinkerwink. (2011, October 31). The zombies of Wal-Mart. *Daily Kos.* Retrieved from http://www.dailykos.com/story/2011/10/31/1031903/-The-Zombies-of-Wal-Mart.

The elements in a citation correspond to the main fields of a record from a search tool. For articles:

- The author is the author(s) of the article
- The title is the title of the article
- The publication information is
  - The title of the periodical or journal
  - Its volume/issue number
  - Its date
  - The page(s) on which the article was published

For books:

- The author is the author(s) or the editor(s) of the book
- The title is the title of the book, including any subtitle
- The publication information is
  - The place of publication (city and sometimes state or country)
  - Publisher
  - Year

All the standard elements of a citation are present in all the examples in Figures 4–5, except for the publication location in 4–5c, the publisher's website example.

Elements Necessary in Any Citation

The parts of each element may be easy to identify (e.g., the author(s) of a book), or more difficult to find (e.g., the individual author of a website). Illustrated in Figure 4–4 are simple directions for creating citations for a book, a periodical article, and a website.

Figure 4–4	Elements of All Citations		
	Books	**Periodical articles**	**Websites and internet**
Author	All authors named; editor(s) usually considered author	All authors named	All authors named, personal or corporate
Title	Complete title, chapter title and complete subtitle	Complete title of article	Title of webpage or website
Publication Information	City, publisher, year of publication	Complete title of periodical, volume and date of periodical, page numbers of article	Date posted, created or updated, date site was retrieved from Web and URL

SKILL CHECK

Find two citations: one from a library catalog and the other from a different search tool. Label the three elements in each that you would use in your citations.

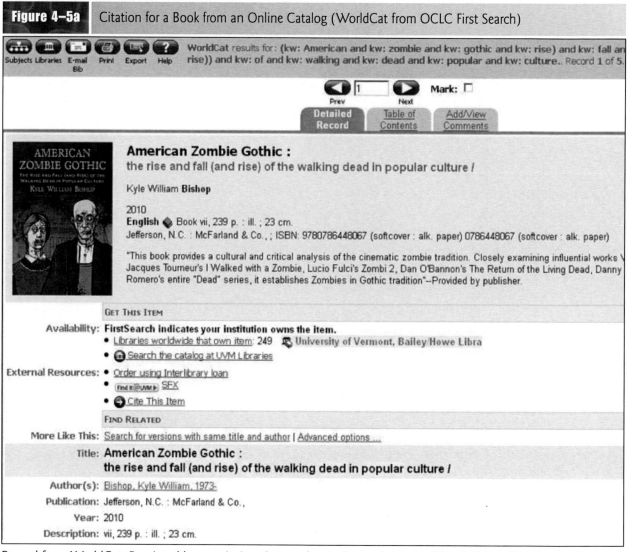

The differences among the various formats are slight but they are important. Use the appropriate style manual and look at *all* the examples it provides for your type of resource (e.g., all the book citation examples or all the periodical article citation examples) so that you can see which examples match your resource most closely. Note also that you will often combine examples from a style manual to a get clear citation for a source you used. Read the text in addition to looking at the examples because the text most often includes the information applicable to resources that differ from the examples. The most important part of creating a list of citations is to include all the basic elements and to be consistent in your format. There is a bibliography at the end of this textbook that you may wish to look at as an example.

Citation Help—Online and Personal

There are websites and programs that create citations that are available for free, that you can buy or to which you can subscribe. Your library may have subscriptions to these kinds of tools known as

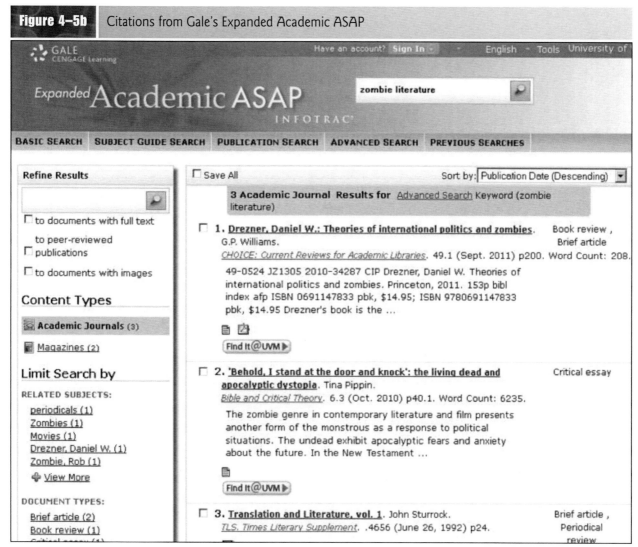

Figure 4–5b Citations from Gale's Expanded Academic ASAP

From Gale. Screen shot from Cengage/Galegroup.com Expanded Academic ASAP. © Gale, a part of Cengage Learning, Inc. Reproduced by permission. www.cengage.com/permissions

bibliographic management software. Some of the more well-established programs include *RefWorks, EndNote, Zotero,* and *Mendeley.* Some of the free online tools are:

- Son of Citation Machine: <http://citationmachine.net/>
- O.P.E.N. (Oregon Public Education Network Clearinghouse) Citation Maker: <http://www. openc.k12.or.us/citeintro/citeintro.php?Grd=3Sec>
- Noodle Tools' NoodleBib Express: <http://www.noodletools.com/login.php>

Such programs are terrific but they may create citations with errors, so use them with care. Be sure to compare the generated citation against a citation manual or check with your course instructor. In addition to providing the bibliographic management software itself, many colleges provide how-to workshops on how to use those programs. Check your campus or your library's website to see if you can get this kind of help.

Figure 4-5c Citation from a Publisher's Website <http://press.princeton.edu/titles/9388.html>

You must know the elements of a citation in order to make citation programs do the work, i.e., you must enter correctly the title of the article and the title of the periodical or the citation will be incorrect. For example, when searching *ProQuest,* the elements in the results list are set up differently from the elements in the records in *Academic Search Premier.*

Personal help in creating or checking your citations is always available. Use the services of your institution's writing lab, and as always, feel free to ask a librarian for help.

ENDNOTES OR FOOTNOTES

The job of the in-text reference is to direct the reader of the research paper to the correct item in your bibliography.

 SEARCH TIP

Remember to look for the "Cite it" or "Export" option in the search tool and follow the directions to generate a formatted citation.

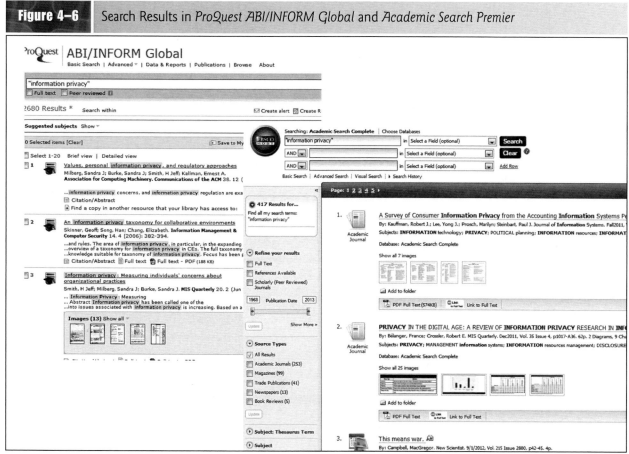

Figure 4–6   Search Results in *ProQuest ABI/INFORM Global* and *Academic Search Premier*

The images and their contents are published with permission of ProQuest LLC. Further reproduction is prohibited without permission.

It is common practice to use a parenthetical reference (MLA) or in-text reference (APA and CSE) to note when you have quoted or paraphrased from a resource. This type of reference makes the reading of your paper smoother than it would be if you used footnotes. The goal of in-text references is to point your reader to the correct resource in the bibliography provided at the end of your paper. The in-text reference must include the first significant word in the citation, because your list of Works Cited or References is in alphabetical order by those first significant words. Check the style manual to be sure what information you must include in an in-text reference. If your professor simply says to "use MLA style" or "use APA style," you can be sure they mean you to use the in-text style of reference with an end-of-paper list of sources used.

If your professor wants you to use footnotes in your paper they usually tell you this explicitly or suggest you follow the "Chicago style"; this is most often the case in History courses.

SKILL CHECK

Can you identify the titles of the periodicals in the citations from Figure 4–6? Are you able to identify the elements in the records from all the databases you have used? Once you know what is what in a database record (a.k.a. citation or reference) you can use programs that make citations for you.

THINKING ABOUT INFORMATION

Most of this book has been designed to help you improve your information research skills. A major component of information literacy is the ability to see information almost as a commodity, a thing that plays a part in all aspects of your learning and life. Citation of information resources of any type acknowledges that you didn't own the information to start with. Ownership of information can be a complex subject. The following discussion simply begins to examine the idea.

OWNERSHIP OF INFORMATION

According to a headline on the Business Software Alliance (BSA) website: "Nationwide Survey Shows most College Students Believe It's Okay to Download Digital Copyrighted Files at School, in Workplace." Colleges have computer policies in place that specifically outlaw such downloads but many students believe the rules to be arbitrary, and argue their own often-tight financial situations justify continuing the practice. Given the global widespread disregard of copyright, should free downloading of all music and movies be legal? Is it possible to own a sound or the rights to a visual story? Who owns what in these situations?

The copyright issue, that is, who owns the right to intellectual property, is a thorny one. Intellectual property, the *American Heritage Dictionary* (2000) tells us, is:

> A product of the intellect that has commercial value, including copyrighted property such as literary or artistic works, and ideational property, such as patents, appellations of origin, business methods, and industrial processes.

Lawyers and business owners have their own opinions on the topic. Law Professor John Tehranian (n.d.) states, "[I]ntellectual property is unlike material property. It is, quite simply, different" (p.5). According to Mitch Bainwol (2004), Chairman, Recording Industry Association of America, "Taking and giving away property that is not yours has enormous economic and creative consequences—lost jobs and lost opportunities for those who create art."

How does one make a product of the intellect into a tangible thing so that ownership can be clearly established? In the past that question was easier to answer. Music, for example, was available only in paper—sheet music, or as a recording—on a vinyl disk, a tape, or a compact disk. Both paper and recordings are tangible things. The company that undertakes the expense of publishing music—making it available for sale to the public—pays royalties to the recording artists. Royalties are a percentage of the profits made after the publisher has paid its recording or publishing expenses, usually based on the number of copies sold. The royalty system applies to published literary works as well.

The computer has made the transfer of content simple and thereby made the question of ownership more difficult. Music or a literary work in digital form resides on a server, and Web users may download it. Information technology is making intellectual property a far less tangible thing. It's out there with billions of other bits and bytes of information, all seemingly accessible for no charge, free, through computers. Free downloads of music, movies, and text generate no profit—no money at all—and therefore the publisher does not pay the performer or writer royalties regardless of the number of downloads.

College students are aware of copyright questions because of the controversy that swirls around music and video downloads. P2P services, such as *Kazaa, LimeWire,* and *Shareaza,* seem to tell students that they can download music for free. You may choose to believe that somehow those services are taking care of the legal questions for them; they are not.

The U.S. Copyright Office states:

> Uploading or downloading works protected by copyright without the authority of the copyright owner is an infringement of the copyright owner's exclusive rights of reproduction and/or distribution. Anyone found to have infringed a copyrighted work may be liable for statutory damages up to $30,000 for each work infringed and, if willful infringement is proven by the copyright owner, that amount may be increased up to $150,000 for each work infringed. In addition, an infringer of a work may also be liable for the attorney's fees incurred by the copyright owner to enforce his or her rights (2006).

Purchase of a song or movie before downloading constitutes receiving "the authority of the copyright owner." And now the artist can be paid.

Organizations such as Broadcast Music Inc. (BMI), and American Society of Composers, Authors, and Publishers (ASCAP) own the copyrights and then issue licenses to radio stations (online and otherwise), performance spaces, etc., to use the copyrighted materials. These groups are currently becoming more aggressive about penalizing those who download illegally. Computer users must realize that keystrokes can be used as cookie crumb trails to track users' activities. Some students have found themselves held accountable by their own colleges for downloading and file sharing because the licensing organizations turned over records of the students' illegal activities to the colleges' IT departments. As mentioned above, most colleges have written policies regarding the college's liability in downloading and in most cases, the policies clearly state that the students themselves will be held accountable for any illegal downloads and will answer to the college's judiciary system.

YouTube.com is another example of the cloudiness of the copyright issue. This website, which allows users to post videos at no charge, has a reputation for trying to stay clean and it regularly seeks out and removes videos that violate copyright law. Rights owners can sign-up to use *YouTube*'s ContentID to help identify compromised videos.

This simple statement from the *YouTube* (2012) website is very clear about how to use the site and avoid any charges of copyright infringement:

> The way to ensure that your video doesn't infringe someone else's copyright is to use your skills and imagination to create something *completely* original. It could be as simple as taping some of your friends goofing around, and as complicated as filming your own short movie with a script, actors, and the whole works. If it's *all* yours, you never have to worry about the copyright—you own it! Make sure to follow the other guidelines in the terms of use, too.

Ownership of information is not just a problem faced in college. Graduating students who move into the worlds of business, science, or the performing arts will be faced with copyright concerns in their fields: patents. Patents (similar to copyrights) on inventions and discoveries are granted, for example, for newly discovered genes or genes altered in a laboratory (science). Ownership of patents is hugely important in businesses such as the pharmaceutical and food processing industries. In the same vein, a newly graduated songwriter (performing arts) may wind up trying to earn a living in a recording industry that has been completely restructured because the royalties-payment structure could no longer survive the widespread piracy by individual downloaders. At this point it's difficult to predict which way copyright law will move. Some in the legal arena suggest that rather than strengthening laws against piracy, corporations should track incidents and use the information to create new markets for products differently handled. Some in the business field foresee more licensing and less selling outright of their products.

Regardless of where copyright law will be in the future, you need to be aware of how it fits into your life now: **everything online is *not* free for everyone.**

But information communicated using the Web can also be vulnerable—to misuse or theft. How secure do you want your personal information to be? Who should guarantee that safety?

Figure 4–7   Cartoonist's Interpretation of the Free Download Situation <www.CartoonStock.com>

"This next block of silence is for all you folks who download music for free, eliminating my incentive to create."

PRIVACY ISSUES

Controlling your personal information in the digital world is critical to your current happiness as well as your future success. Pictures and videos posted to Facebook and YouTube, tweets shared with the world, for example, even when removed from a site still have a life of their own and may reap unintended consequences. Prospective employers routinely search the Web before completing the hiring process: be careful of how you manage your online image.

Personal data is incredibly valuable. Have you noticed that the advertisements appearing on your favorite websites are tailored to searches you have recently conducted? This is no accident; cookies provide businesses with a wealth of information:

> Advertising networks use cookies to keep track of ads they have already shown to a user. They can control the ads they show to a user based on a parameters such as the page the user is downloading, the number of times the user has seen a particular ad, the time of day, etc. <http://www.silicon-press.com/briefs/brief.cookiead/index.html> (Kristol, n.d.)

Privacy policies posted on many websites, such as on Amazon's website, indicate: "Amazon.com knows that you care how information about you is used and shared, and we appreciate your trust that we will do so carefully and sensibly." This is not about keeping your credit card number secure, this is about tracking your habits as a consumer. What is careful and sensible to Amazon may or may not be careful and sensible to you.

Identity theft is another important information issue. The Federal Trade Commission (FTC) states that identity theft:

> [O]ccurs when someone uses your personal information such as your name, Social Security number, credit card number or other identifying information, without your permission, to commit fraud or other crimes.

The FTC provides this definition and a wealth of information about identity theft at their Identity Theft Site <http://www.ftc.gov/bcp/edu/microsites/idtheft/>. The advent of information technology has made the illegal use of one's personal information easier than in the past. There have been numerous news reports of employees stealing personal information from their employers' data banks and sometimes selling the information to other users worldwide. Other theft occurs when criminals use approaches such as pretexting, phishing, and spoofing, explained on the next pages.

Pretexting, Phishing, and Spoofing

Pretexting is a method of getting personal information under false pretenses. An identity thief pretends to be you, for example, in a phone call to your bank. A good pretexter can obtain account numbers and balances without your knowledge, much less your consent. The amount of information available on social networks has dramatically increased the risk posed by pretexting.

Phishing and spoofing are online activities related to fraud schemes. Phishing involves e-mails sent from what appear to be legitimate online businesses, often those that you have used. The e-mails ask for information to verify your account or a similar ruse; the information requested is sensitive personal information such as account numbers. The mimicry of legitimate Web sites such as *eBay* or *PayPal* is impressive.

Companies that are portrayed in phishing scams often protect themselves by giving their members clues to distinguish fake e-mails from legitimate ones. For example, some companies tell their members to look for their own names in the messages; phishing e-mails will not use a personal name because they're generated by hackers who do not have access to the members' names.

Spoofing is the assumption of another's identity, again often in e-mails that appear to be sent from a company or agency that you use or are familiar with, perhaps asking you to change a password for an online account. Firewalls (see the *Glossary*) can help prevent you from becoming a victim of spoofing.

One victim of identity theft discovered that the thief obtained a photocopy of her driver's license from a non-shredded trash basket. Her employer had required the copy of her license; when she updated it with a copy of her new license, the old copy was carelessly discarded. The thief then obtained credit cards in the victim's name and started spending. The theft was discovered when a credit card company called the victim to ask why she was opening a second account. She was lucky; the thief was caught and prosecuted. The credit card companies used by the thief did not charge the victim; they absorbed the loss, but this may have been because the amounts were relatively low.

CONCEPT CHECK

Identity theft is a crime in many states and in some instances it can be a federal crime. Does your state have an identity theft law?

The ID theft victim above was certainly not responsible for being careless in making her personal information available. Can you say the same?

The number of victims of identity theft is rising. In 2010, 250,854 people made identity theft complaints (Federal Trade Commission, 2011, March 8). The most common use of stolen information was credit card fraud. An indication of the gravity of the situation is the increasing number of companies that offer subscription services for everything from protection from identity theft to insurance that guarantees some measure of financial reimbursement to theft victims. The best way to protect yourself, according to the FTC, is to be aware of your personal information: how much is in your bank account(s), the amount *you* have charged on your credit card(s), what your various passwords are and where you store that information. Monitor your information often and report immediately any suspicious activity in any of your accounts to the appropriate company.

While businesses are looking for ways to prevent such schemes and make all transactions as secure as possible—with computer hackers unceasingly working to break through their tightest and newest security programs—the questions for you are:

Is *your* information safe, and how can *you* ensure that it is?

This is a new responsibility for many, one brought to life by the ubiquity of online services and activities.

Privacy Protection versus Freedom of Information Access

We relish the convenience of online financial transactions, from buying a book to trading shares of stock to paying all bills electronically through online connections to banking. With that convenience is a proportional risk to our privacy. In this post-9/11 world, many are willing to share personal information for personal safety goals—with airlines and airports, for example—but may not be willing to share as much information in order to do their banking online.

A survey from *ComputerWorld* revealed that "individuals view their right to privacy as increasingly important and worry about how organizations collect, use and share their personal information. Other concerns include . . . loss of civil liberties" (Ponemon, 2004).

Information technology is highlighting a line that individuals may have thought did not exist in their own lives: the line between privacy and intrusion. Who has the right to require you to provide what information about yourself? The opposite of this may be the limits imposed on access to information, such as situations that arise because of the Health Information Portability and Accountability Act (often called HIPAA), a U.S. law related to health information and privacy. If you need medical treatment in an emergency situation, this law will directly affect you because it may be difficult for a relative to discover which hospital is treating you; hospitals are not allowed to give anyone that information without your consent.

Does any government have the right to demand that you allow it to share your personal information? On the other hand, does any government have the right to require your information to be

---

SKILL CHECK

There are many websites that provide help in how to protect your information. Go to the FTC site mentioned above, or do a search under "identity theft" and privacy. List two new things you learned about protecting your identity.

withheld, even in emergency situations? Again the question is yours to answer. The American Civil Liberties Union (2012) includes on its website this statement on the first page of the section devoted to *Privacy and Technology:*

> The Technology & Liberty Project monitors the interplay between cutting-edge technology and civil liberties, actively promoting responsible uses of technology that enhance privacy and freedom, while opposing those that undermine our freedoms and move us closer to a surveillance society.

Your reaction to this statement could begin a lively discussion of privacy rights and technological advances. Laws are written and passed by those you elect. You can influence their stands and choices, or you can choose not to. One benefit of a free society is that its citizens choose their level of involvement in the running of that society and help set limits on surveillance and privacy.

Ethical Use of Information

Information technology makes physical (or virtual/digital) access easier to all sorts of information. It raises the thorny issue of ethical use of information once it has been accessed.

There is a Media Ethics Division of the Association for Education in Journalism and Mass Communication. Each year at the Association's convention, members of the Division present several papers on the ethical use of information. The topics of the papers provide a glimpse of the issues with which media reporters—for print publications, television/radio news organizations, and online resources—grapple. How much information is TMI—too much information? Whose information should be made public; that is, does a public figure have fewer rights to privacy than the non-famous ordinary person? Should they have fewer rights?

It is not just those who write or report the news who have to face the issue of ethical use of information. Plagiarism at any level, from student papers to professional media publications, is unethical use of information. Some well-known situations that might raise questions of ethical use include media coverage of Whitney Houston, both in life and surrounding her death; the leak of a CIA operative's identity, possibly as retaliation for a political statement by her spouse; Bernard Madoff's Ponzi scheme, which landed him in jail; pharmaceutical companies reporting only favorable results of drug trials. The list could go on.

How information can or should be used will be argued for the foreseeable future. Who should or can set the standards for ethical use will also be debated for a long time to come. How will this affect you? You may have to choose whether to use an incident that occurred between you and your roommate as an example in a paper. Or you may have to decide whether to tell a family member what you learned by accident about their medical situation. You might be tempted to alter your resume with exaggerated work experience or enhanced job titles. Or you see an e-mail to your younger sibling that indicates that they are involved in potentially dangerous online activities; do you share that information with your parents?

Information surrounds you and you need to sort through the vast amounts of it. You need to understand how to use that information so that the information does no damage and is used to its— and your—best advantage. As well, you need to protect your private information.

Social Networking Sites

An issue that falls into both the privacy field and the ethical use of information is that of social networking. A problem with *Facebook, Twitter,* or *GooglePlus* is that many users think they are communicating (i.e., sharing information) with their friends only, when in reality the sites provide easy access to everyone. Prospective employers now routinely search for applicants' pages on such sites; a recent graduate who is a candidate for a job may have unknowingly jeopardized the chance to obtain that position by posting evidence of behavior that doesn't meet the standards of the potential employer.

Is such use of personal information ethical on the part of the employer? The student posted it to be seen by friends, not realizing it would be viewed by strangers. Should the student self-censor information that might put them in a bad light? The employer is not an expected user of such sites so the student might argue that the employer has no rights to this information. Obviously there will be strong arguments on both sides of this type of question.

When using the Web, it may be best to take a cautious approach, to behave as if everything is accessible by everyone. This applies to social networking sites, personal Web cams, blogs, virtually everything you post on any website. Remember that you may be seeing a few known friends as your audience when you may actually have the world looking in your window.

Figure 4-8   Example of a Social Networking Site, *Facebook*

CENSORSHIP

Before delving into an examination of censorship we should look again at bias in information resources. There is an introduction to the concept of bias in Chapter 3 that should be reviewed as part of any censorship discussion. Princeton University's online dictionary *WordNet* (n.d.) defines bias (as a noun) as "a partiality that prevents objective consideration of an issue or situation." Any highly charged topic can provide an example of such partiality. For example, look at the two images and headlines about the BP oil spill settlement in Figures 4–9 and 4–10.

News organizations are allowed to select one perspective when reporting. They are not obligated to consider all points of view; that is bias, not censorship. However, if a website, WikiLeaks for instance, were to be removed or eliminated because it is deemed offensive or a threat to national security that would be censorship.

A common type of censorship is the removal of a book from a library, especially a school library, because some parents object to its content. *Banned Books Week* is an anti-censorship awareness campaign promoted by the American Library Association (<http://www.ala.org/advocacy/banned/bannedbooksweek>).

Figure 4–9   Website from Fox Business News Covering the BP Oil Spill Settlement

<http://www.foxbusiness.com/industries/2012/04/18/bp-oil-spill-plaintiffs-hammer-out-settlement>

Figure 4–10 Website from CNN Covering the BP Oil Spill Settlement http://articles.cnn.com/2012–04–18/us/us_bp-spill-settlement_1_bp-estimates-deepwater-horizon-gulf-oil-disaster?_s=PM:US

Scenario

A college librarian asked her students to go to the website of a white supremacy organization, using it as a discussion-starter. The issue under discussion was censorship. The students were all planning to become elementary and secondary school teachers. This is the scenario posed by the librarian:

You teach a class to sixth graders who are, on average, 12 years old. You have talked about slavery, the U.S. Civil War, and the slow development of civil rights in the U.S. You ask your students to go to the website and decide whether organizations such as this should "be allowed" to be accessible by anyone. The students do a good job of offering opinions and reasons and you feel the exercise was a success. The next day a furious parent appears at the close of the school day and demands that you accompany them to the principal's office so they can describe what their child said about yesterday's class. The parents want you fired for showing such material to sixth grade students; his child simply said they went to this "cool" site yesterday. (The graphics at the site were impressive.)

How would the education students handle this state of affairs?

The education students had never thought about this type of situation. In their view the Web was not a place where censorship belonged. The students were divided about whether it was wise

SKILL CHECK

Find three books that are on a current list of banned books.

for the hypothetical teacher to show such a website to students of that age. And the discussion easily broadened to address students of any age, and then whether anyone, parents or governments, should be able to dictate which websites were off limits. Censorship was hitting home.

In homes where children watch television and routinely go online, parents may impose censorship through the use of blocking technology. Parents may decide to filter what their children are able to access in their own homes; that is a private decision. Censorship on a public level is a different situation because it involves someone—a committee, a political body, an individual—dictating what is and is not available to all.

Public and school libraries in the United States, in order to receive federal funding to support Internet connections, are required to install filters on their computers so that patrons do not have access to child pornography, obscene materials, or information that may be considered harmful to minors. The Children's Internet Protection Act or CIPA is the law passed in 2000 that requires filters. Some libraries decided to forego federal money and have not installed filters. Many other libraries depend heavily on federal financing to stay open and have installed the filters. The American Library Association, always at the forefront of censorship issues, opposed CIPA and sued, testing the law's constitutionality. The U.S. Supreme Court ruled CIPA constitutional so that libraries must comply or lose the federal subsidies for their ISPs (Internet Service Providers).

Some believe that requiring web filters on computers in public libraries violates the First Amendment to the U.S. Constitution. It is argued that filters block many sites that do not have any of the type of content described above. A site on breast cancer is not pornography but the word "breast" may cause it to be blocked by a public library's filter. Can students do research on race horses if access to race tracks is denied by their school library's filters because gambling sites may be dangerous to children? The law makes provisions for individual users to request that filters be removed while they are using a computer; many patrons are loath to make such a request because of the personal information they must divulge in order to do so.

Is CIPA censorship in the same way that it is censorship for a parents' group to demand removal of the often-banned book, *The Bluest Eye* by Toni Morrison, from their high school library? Should the government—from the public library board and the school district level all the way to the U.S. Congress and courts—be allowed to impose filters? Whose responsibility is it to ensure that children have no access to websites someone finds undesirable: parents or schools or libraries or . . .? For more information about filters, go to a website such as *Internet-filters.net* but keep in mind what you now know about bias.

The Web has been described as the great democratizer of information, allowing access by anyone to anything. Is that view accurate today? Should open access to everything be a policy enforced by governments? These questions raise another information issue, that of the digital divide.

THE DIGITAL DIVIDE

Before the invention of the printing press in 1455, information was owned by those who had access to the hand-written or wooden block-printed books most often produced, in the Western world, by

CONCEPT CHECK

The Electronic Frontier Foundation (EFF), an organization devoted to issues of online privacy and freedom, began a campaign in the late 1990s to label websites that support efforts to keep access open. What are some other issues related to privacy and censorship on their website, https://www.eff.org/?

| **Figure 4–11** | Household Internet Usage and Family Income |

Table 1155. Household Internet Usage In and Outside of the Home by Selected Characteristics: 2010

[In percent, except as indicated. As of October. Internet Use Supplement 2010. Excludes GPS devices, digital music players, and devices with only limited computing capabilities, for example: household appliances. Based on the Current Population Survey. See text, Section 1 and Appendix III]

Characteristics	Total households (1,000)	In the home			Anywhere		No internet use	
		Percent			Total households (1,000)	Percent of households	Total households (1,000)	Percent of households
		All households	Dial-Up	Broadband				
Bachelors degree or more	36,251	89.24	2.07	87.17	34,014	93.83	2,238	6.17
Family Income of householder \1								
Less than $15,000	15,369	39.58	2.87	36.71	8,797	57.24	6,572	42.76
15,000 to 24,999	11,116	52.61	3.40	49.21	7,380	66.39	3,736	33.61
25,000 to 34,999	11,971	63.27	3.38	59.89	9,097	75.99	2,874	24.01
35,000 to 49,999	13,333	77.88	3.37	74.51	11,615	87.11	1,718	12.89
50,000 to 74,999	16,391	87.14	2.83	84.31	15,327	93.51	1,064	6.49
75,000 to 99,999	9,785	93.84	2.13	91.71	9,513	97.22	272	2.78
100,000 to 149,000	8,685	96.38	1.57	94.81	8,531	98.22	154	1.78
150,000 and over	5,961	97.99	0.68	97.31	5,899	98.97	61	1.03

FOOTNOTE
\1 Includes other groups not shown seperately
Source: U.S. Department of Commerce, National Telecommunications and Information Administration, "Digital Nation: Expanding Internet Usage," February 2011, <http://www.ntia.doc.gov/reports.html>.
For more information:
http://www.ntia.doc.gov/data
Internet release date: 9/30/2011

the Catholic Church. Access was understandably quite limited and as a result, ownership of information ensured power in the hands of the owners. The wealthy minority of the population was aware of the news, ideas, and concepts passed through the printed word; the poorer people had to take as truth information given to them by the minority, with no chance to know if there might be different interpretations of events. There was a clear divide between the information-haves and -have-nots.

The divide now is a digital one. The digital divide refers to the fact that some people have ready access to computers and information while others do not. The OECD (Organisation for Economic Co-operation and Development) defines the phrase as one that:

> [R]efers to the gap that exists in the opportunities to access advanced information and communication technologies between geographic areas or by individuals at different socio-economic levels (2002).

On one side of the divide are the haves, those who have computers and are able to use them frequently with few impediments. The have-nots are on the other side of the divide with restricted or no access to computers and information that is available only electronically.

Globally, nations that are less economically developed are the have-nots while countries higher on the economic ladder are the haves. Within a country, the United States, for example, the haves are in a higher socioeconomic level while the have-nots are the poorer citizens. These statistics in Figure 4–11 are from the U.S. Census Bureau, published in the *Statistical Abstract of the United States: 2012.*

Do numbers such as these indicate a trend in which lower-income citizens have less information and therefore less power? The question is yours to address.

Have-nots live in worlds where information—because it is online—is limited because access to it is limited or non-existent.

A hypothetical warfare situation illustrates the dangers of unequal access to information and communications technology (ICT). An army that has limited access to ICT will be at the mercy of

Figure 4-12	Graphical Illustration of the Internet Users World Wide by Region

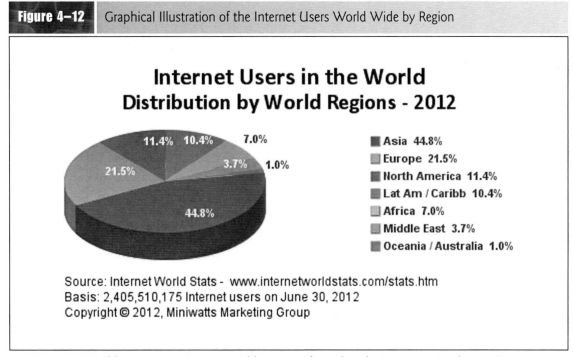

Internet Users in the World
Distribution by World Regions - 2012

- Asia 44.8%
- Europe 21.5%
- North America 11.4%
- Lat Am / Caribb 10.4%
- Africa 7.0%
- Middle East 3.7%
- Oceania / Australia 1.0%

Source: Internet World Stats - www.internetworldstats.com/stats.htm
Basis: 2,405,510,175 Internet users on June 30, 2012
Copyright © 2012, Miniwatts Marketing Group

From Internet World Stats, www.internetworldstats.com/stats.htm by Miniwatts Marketing Group.
Copyright © 2012 by Miniwatts Marketing Group. Reprinted by permission.

one with more access. Why? Because the second army will be better able to coordinate its movements and to know where the first army is by using ICT. The first army will be fighting largely in the dark with limited knowledge and therefore limited abilities to coordinate efforts.

You may not realize how privileged you are compared to the rest of the world. You think nothing of going to your own computer and getting immediately almost any information you need. Take a medical question, for example. You turned your ankle playing touch football. You go to *WebMD*, review the symptoms of sprains and breaks, and make a decision to wrap the ankle and not get it checked. Regardless of the wisdom of the choice, the fact that you had the information at your fingertips allowed you to make that decision. A person in a less economically developed country would not only not have access to *WebMD*, they would not have a computer and there might not be a constant supply of electricity. Their medical condition would remain unknown. According to John Mitchell (n.d.) from the *Center for Media Literacy:*

> Everyone knows information is a form of power. The Third World countries now know this more than ever. That is why they are calling for the establishment of a new international order of information. They feel this is just as urgent as the establishment of a new international economic order.

CONCEPT CHECK

Those who have computers and access to the Internet and the Web have become new haves in many societies. Who are the haves and the have-nots in your community?

The statement above supports the reality that individuals in less wired countries who have limited access to political as well as medical information may be at the mercy of the party with the best ICT. Open, free, and easy access to information helps to quell rumors and to level political playing fields. Countries with a higher level of ICT will advance economically faster than those with a lower level. Economically developing countries will have to decide how much of their (often very limited) budgets they can spend on ICT. That decision will affect their spending on other necessities; health care, for example. The question of readily available access to information and communication and their technologies will deeply affect development in all countries.

CONCEPT CHECK

How do the events of the Arab Spring of 2011 influence your thinking about the connection between economic empowerment and political change?

CHAPTER HIGHLIGHTS

■ There are broad social and ethical questions raised by information and IT use.

■ Ownership of information includes questions of copyright that apply to (seemingly) free downloading of music and videos, and to cutting and pasting information from websites.

■ Everything online is not free.

■ Plagiarism relates to ownership of information because it is a theft of information or intellectual property and ideas. It is plagiarism to turn in a paper as one's own after purchasing or obtaining it through exchange from a paper mill site.

■ Privacy issues relevant to information and IT include privacy rights and identity theft through pretexting, phishing, and spoofing.

■ Ethical use of information involves questions of what and who is public and what privacy rights are accorded to them.

■ Social networking sites such as *Facebook* should be used with care because of privacy and ethical use issues.

■ You must consciously use information as it should best be used.

■ Censorship limits access to information. It is difficult for any one person or organization to speak for everyone regarding what information should or should not be accessible in books and all other media, including the Web.

■ Unequal access to information and communications technology (ICT) has created a digital divide.
   ● Groups with more access usually include the more economically developed regions and countries.
   ● Within a country there is a digital divide between:
   ● The more affluent who have more access to computers and more access to information because they have a higher rate of Internet connectivity.
       ■ People in lower socioeconomic levels who have fewer computers and less communications technology or those in rural or geographically hard to reach areas and have less communications technology and thus more restricted access to information.
       ■ Because information is power, there may be political danger in a widening digital divide.

CHAPTER 4

Questions

1. There are ethical and legal considerations when doing research. Plagiarism at any level, from student papers to professional media publications, is unethical use of information. Explain what creating good citations has to do with plagiarism.

2. Technology makes accessing and downloading music, video, and literary works in digital format easy. What is copyright and whose responsibility is it to protect copyright? Explain your answer.

3. Information technology is highlighting a line that individuals may have thought did not exist in their own lives: the line between privacy and intrusion. How do you control and protect your personal information? Who has the right to require you to provide what information about yourself? Please explain your answer.

Glossary

(Some terms listed below will not be found in the text.)

Nearly all subject areas and disciplines, professions and crafts have their own languages or jargon. The field of information research and technology is no exception; it has its own words and phrases that are used frequently. Below is a glossary of some of these terms. The definitions are intentionally non-scientific and are addressed to you as an information and technology user. The words and initialisms are used by people with experience in doing information research.

abstracting service: a search tool that's published regularly that provides subject access to information by means of abstracts and indexes; abstracting services provide abstracts, which are "abbreviated, accurate representations of works, usually without added interpretation or criticism." (Young 1)

annotated bibliography: a list of citations of information sources—the *bibliography*—where each citation includes a short description of the information source—the *annotation.*

apps, applications: "Application is short for application program, which is a program designed to perform a specific function. Examples include cell phone and iPad apps, word processors, Web browsers, database tools, and graphics programs." An **applet** is a little application that does one job, such as animating an object on a Web page.

bandwidth: a measure of the rate at which data can be transferred electronically. Bandwidth is used in descriptions of Internet connection devices, such as, "A modem connection is narrow bandwidth while a DSL connection is broadband."

bibliographic record: information about an information source (e.g., a book, a recording, etc.) that completely identifies the source—its title, author(s), and publishing information—provided in a standardized form, such as a record in a database for a book or a periodical article.

bibliography: "a list of works, documents, and/or bibliographic items, usually with some relationship among them e.g., by a given author [or] on a given subject." (Young 22)

blog: "(short for weblog) is a personal online journal that's frequently updated and intended for general public consumption." (WhatIs.com)

Boolean searching: use of logical operators to conduct a search. Boolean searching allows the user to search for several concepts at once by specifying that all, some, or none of the concepts be represented in every item retrieved. Boolean operators used in research are AND, NOT, and OR.

bound periodical: issues comprising volumes of a periodical that have been put together and given a hard cover; for example, the issues of volume 18, 1996, of Women's Sports and Fitness are bound into one physical volume. Bound volumes of periodicals are kept separate from unbound issues and microform volumes of periodicals in many libraries.

bps: bits per second. This is a measurement of how fast information travels to your computer from your ISP; the higher the number the faster the transmission and therefore your access to the information on-line. For example, 57.6 Kbps using a modem connection results in a greater download time for a Web page than a DSL or cable connection—see later—that delivers 512 Kbps or more (that's K for kilo or 1,000 bits per second).

browser: another word for client. Some frequently used Web browsers are *Apple Safari, Internet Explorer, Mozilla Firefox,* and *Google Chrome.*

browsing: reading titles in the book stacks of a library.

call number: the number assigned to an item in an information collection to indicate its location, most often based on the subject content of the item. A call number might be compared to a house number as part of an address.

catalog: "a file of bibliographic records, created according to specific and uniform principles of construction … which describes the materials contained in a collection [or] library." (Young 37)

CD: an initialism for Compact Disk that's one format for electronic information. Data is stored and searched digitally on a compact disk using a personal computer with compatible software.

cite: "to quote as an authority or example; to mention as support, illustration, or proof." (*American Heritage Dictionary*)

click on: the action you take to activate a link or a button on the screen of a computer. You may use a mouse to move the cursor to a link or a button (usually an icon) and then press the mouse button (click).

client-server: an interaction between a user and a computer that works this way, according to the "Internet Glossary" at the *MacintoshOS* Web site: "When you and your computer are searching for or accessing information on another computer, you are the client. The other computer is the server, and together you are using client/server technology. The server stores the info and makes it available to all authorized clients." Your client to use the Web may be the *Netscape Navigator* browser; the Web is the protocol it uses.

cloud computing: a specific type of client-server interaction, where most of your documents and data are stored in a remote server that you access from wherever you are working. Gmail is one example of a common cloud computing service. Clouds can be public and open to anyone or private and restricted for one company or organization to use.

collections (in a library):   a group of materials kept together. Examples of collections that are common to many libraries include:

General or Circulating Collection: books, some of which come with CD's or other included materials, that circulate to (can be checked out by) the library's authorized users

Media Collection: a group of materials that are for the most part non-print, housed with or near their appropriate equipment

Reference Collection: information sources that provide brief authoritative information and search tools that provide reference to other sources, kept together in one area of a library and usually not allowed to circulate

Periodicals Collection: magazines, journals, and newspapers in all their formats: unbound issues, bound volumes, and issues and volumes in microformats—microfilm and microfiche, usually kept in an area of a library apart from the general collection

Special Collections: "collections of library materials separated from the general collection because they are of a certain form, on a certain subject, of a certain period or geographical area, rare, fragile or valuable." (Young 211) Examples of special collections are a local history collection, donated papers from a local luminary, college archives, etc.

computer: "A device that computes, esp. an electronic machine that performs high-speed mathematical or logical calculations or that assembles, stores, correlates, or otherwise processes and prints information derived from coded data in accordance with a predetermined program." (*American Heritage Dictionary*) Please note that the definition does NOT include the word "think" anywhere!

controlled vocabulary indexing system: "an indexing system in which the indexer, in assigning descriptors to works, is limited to a specified list of terms called the index vocabulary." (Young 59)

cross-reference: a direction from one subject heading or descriptor to another.

cookies: "A cookie is a piece of text that a Web server can store on a user's hard disk. Cookies allow a Web site to store information on a user's machine and later retrieve it." Go to the source of this definition, HowStuffWorks.com for an explanation of what cookies do.

cursor: an icon that's usually a flashing rectangle, a vertical line, or an arrow, plain or somewhat stylized, that indicates where action will take place on the computer screen. The mouse or the arrow keys manipulate the cursor.

database: "A **database** is an organized collection of data, today typically in digital form. The data are typically organized to model relevant aspects of reality (for example, the availability of rooms in hotels), in a way that supports processes requiring this information (for example, finding a hotel with vacancies)." So says *Wikipedia, The Free Encyclopedia* <http://en.wikipedia.org/wiki/database>. **Librarians often refer to any computerized index as a database; usually they mean those bibliographic databases that they can access because their institutions pay subscription fees.** Most bibliographic databases provide periodical literature, or references to the articles in periodicals, as well as materials other than periodicals such as book chapters, or references to them.

default: "selection automatically used by a computer program in the absence of a choice made by the user." *Merriam Webster Online*

descriptor: a term used to describe the subject content of an information source; also called a subject heading.

directory (a.k.a. Internet subject directory or Web directory): good beginning point for Web research. A Web directory is constructed by a person who has reviewed Web sites and chosen those he or she considers worth exploring, and organizes the selections, most often by subject.

download: to bring to your computer or to a floppy disk information that's on another computer.

DSL (Digital Subscriber Line): "a technology for bringing high-bandwidth information to homes and small businesses over ordinary copper telephone lines." <http://searchwin2000.techtarget.com/sDefinition/0,,sid1_gci212964,00.html>

DVD (Digital Versatile Disc): "an optical disc storage format, invented and developed by Philips, Sony, Toshiba, and Panasonic in 1995. DVDs offer higher storage capacity than Compact Discs while having the same dimensions." Wikipedia, The Free Encyclopedia <http://en.wikipedia.org/wiki/DVD>.

e-mail: electronic mail. E-mail is a means of communicating with another person using the Internet.

embargo: "In the world of electronic databases of periodicals this term refers to the practice of publishers whereby they hold back recent issues of the print version of their periodicals from electronic databases. The reason is that the immediate release of the publications to electronic databases would reduce the sale of the print periodicals. Periodicals can be held back for a period ranging from a week to over a year. Each database usually provides information about the length of embargo for its publications." This definition is from Oakland Community College's Library Tutorial on Finding Articles. <http://oaklandcc. edu/library/searchpath/Module4/01c_journals.html>.

field: part of a record of an information source; "a defined subdivision of a record used to record only a specific category of data," (Young 92), for example, data about the author(s) comprises the author field.

field tag: the abbreviation used by a search tool, usually in electronic form, to identify a field; also called field label.

firewall: "A system designed to prevent unauthorized access to or from a private network. Firewalls can be implemented in both hardware and software, or a combination of both. Firewalls are frequently used to prevent unauthorized Internet users from accessing private networks connected to the Internet, especially intranets. All messages entering or leaving the intranet pass through the firewall, which examines each message and blocks those that do not meet the specified security criteria." <http://www.webopedia.com/ TERM/F/firewall.html>.

hardware: the physical components of a computer; i.e., the keyboard, CPU, monitor, modem, and any other physical pieces that make up a computer.

hits: matches made by the computer in a search. Each item on the list of retrieved records is a "hit."

Home Page: the beginning or "home" screens of a Web resource. A Home Page is somewhat like the title page of a book in that it's the starting point for that resource, even though you may use the resource without ever going to its Home Page.

HTML: HyperText Markup Language, the computer language used to make information readable at many Web sites. Other languages also are currently in use; e.g., XML and SGML.

http: hypertext transfer protocol, which is what is used to display the information that's written in HTML. A URL, or address on the Web, most commonly begins <http://> to let the computer know that the information at the Web site is in hypertext format.

https: By convention, URLs that require an SSL (Short for *Secure Sockets Layer,* a protocol developed by Netscape for transmitting private documents via the Internet) connection start with *https:* instead of *http.*

<http://www.webopedia.com/TERM/S/SSL.html>

Look for this whenever you are entering password or personal financial or health information into a website.

hypertext: a term coined by Ted Nelson in 1964 that refers to text that includes links to other information sources. Hypertext allows a user to move in a non-linear fashion through information sources.

icon: a picture on a computer that represents a category or file of information, and may be clicked on to connect to that information.

index: a systematic guide to the contents of an information source. An index consists of descriptors or other words or symbols (such as report numbers) representing the contents, and references (such as page numbers) for accessing the contents of the source. (Young 116)

information system: an organized structure of interrelated information sources; for example, a library's collections, or a library catalog.

Instant Messaging: "Abbreviated *IM,* a type of communications service that enables you to create a kind of private chat room with another individual in order to communicate in real time over the Internet, analagous to a telephone conversation but using text-based, not voice-based, communication. Typically, the instant messaging system alerts you whenever somebody on your private list is online. You can then initiate a chat session with that particular individual." <http://www.webopedia.com/TERM/I/instant_messaging.html>

Internet: a network of computer networks throughout the world; i.e., international. The Internet is often referred to as "the Net." The phrase "surfing the Net" means exploring sites; i.e., viewing the information available on computers connected through this network.

journal: a periodical that contains scholarly information or current information on research and development whose intended audience includes scholars, practitioners, and experts in the subject field covered by the publication. A periodical does not have to include the word journal in its title to be considered a journal. Compare to the definition of "magazine."

LC: abbreviation for "Library of Congress."

link(s): connection(s) to other Web resources provided at a Web site. Links are usually underlined and of a color different from the rest of the text on a screen. They may also be icons. When you use a mouse, you will see the cursor's arrow change to a pointing finger when the mouse positions the cursor over a link.

listserv: an electronic mailing list used for communication purposes, set up such that a subscriber sends a message to a central point and the message is then distributed to all other subscribers who read and react to it. The best listservs are moderated, that is, a designated person screens all messages sent "to the list" and distributes only those that relate to the subject matter to which the list is dedicated.

magazine: weekly, biweekly, or monthly periodical that's intended for a general readership, usually with articles on various topics by different authors. (Some periodicals that include the world journal in their titles actually are magazines.) Compare to the definition of "journal."

microfiche: one type of microformat that's flat sheets of film containing micro-images of periodicals or books arranged in a grid pattern; see also "microfilm."

microfilm: one type of microformat that is roll film containing micro-images of periodicals or books; see also "microfiche."

modem: communications device that converts the digital data from a computer into analog format that can be transmitted over telephone lines; short for modulator/demodulator.

nonprint media (sometimes called audiovisual materials): materials in audio and visual formats such as film and tape that convey information primarily by sound and image rather than by text, now also incorporating digitally stored information on compact disks with sound and visual recordings.

online: accessible through a computer, such as an online database. Sometimes this term is used instead of "electronic" or "digitally stored."

opac: a name sometimes given to a library's online catalog. It's actually an acronym that stands for Online Public Access Catalog.

operating system (OS): the basic computer programming used by a computer to work with various programs or software. The *American Heritage Dictionary* definition is: "Software designed to control the hardware of a specific data-processing system in order to allow users and application programs to make use of it." <http://ahdictionary.com/word/search.html?q5operating1system> Examples of operating systems are Windows and Windows XP. Mac OS X is the operating system for Apple computers. Also part of the field are Linux and BSD, Unix-type OSs that are available for free download from the Web.

P2P (peer-to-peer):   "File-sharing (more specifically, 'peer-to-peer file-sharing' or 'P2P') is in simple terms a way for people connected to the Internet to share files stored on their computers. File-sharing services such as *Kazaa, Grokster, Morpheus, i-Mesh,* etc. provide software which enables people to search for files on other people's computers." This definition is from *Tech Terms Computer Dictionary* which provides more information about file-sharing at <http://www.copyrightguru.com/file_sharing_faq.htm>.

periodical: a publication that's published at regular intervals of more than one day (i.e., periodically), usually referring to magazines, journals, and newspapers.

peripheral(s):   "A computer device, such as a CD-ROM drive or printer, that is not part of the essential computer; i.e., the memory and microprocessor. Peripheral devices can be external—such as a mouse, keyboard, printer, monitor, external Zip drive, or scanner—or internal, such as a CD-ROM drive, CD-R drive, or internal modem. Internal peripheral devices are often referred to as *integrated peripherals*. Webopedia <http://webopedia.com/>.

phishing: "Phishing is a form of criminal activity using social engineering techniques through email or instant messaging. Phishers attempt to fraudulently acquire other people's personal information, such as passwords and credit card details, by masquerading as a trustworthy person or business in an apparently official electronic communication." McAffee, a company that sells virus protection software, provided this definition in its Virus Glossary at <http://home.mcafee.com/virusinfo>.

portal: "a Web site or service that offers a broad array of resources and services, such as e-mail, forums, search engines, and on-line shopping malls. The first Web portals were online services, such as AOL, that provided access to the Web, but by now most of the traditional search engines have transformed themselves into Web portals to attract and keep a larger audience." This is according to Webopedia <http://webopedia.com/>.

protocol: " A set of rules that determines how data is sent back and forth between two applications," according to the "Internet Glossary" at the *MacintoshOS* Web site. <http://www.apple.com/quicktime/pdf/QT_Streaming_Server_v10.4.pdf>

record: an entry in a search tool (paper or electronic) that provides enough information about an information source to completely identify the source, arranged in a standardized form. A record includes author, title, and publishing information.

search engine: software used to search through the myriad sites on the World Wide Web. A search engine works much like an electronic index does, searching through sites on the Internet for matches to the strings of letters (words) you type in. Items retrieved include the URL for each Web site.

search statement: a series of search terms combined to describe an information need and designed to be usable in a particular search tool. For example, a search statement that could be used in a library's catalog for information about the Lake Champlain monster is *Lake Champlain AND sea monsters.*

search term: a single word, multiple-word phrase, or significant number (e.g., report number or law number), used to search for information. A search term is the term you look under (type) in a search tool.

server: "1) In information technology, a server is a computer program that provides services to other computer programs (and their users) in the same or other computers. 2) The computer that a server program runs in is also frequently referred to as a server (though it may be used for other purposes as well). ... Specific to the Web, a Web server is the computer program (housed in a computer) that serves requested HTML pages or files. A Web *client* is the requesting program associated with the user. The Web browser in your computer is a client that requests HTML files from Web servers." "Server." WhatIs.com Terms. <http://whatis.techtarget.com/definition/0,,sid9_gci212964,00.html>

set: in information research, a group of records in a database that share a common element, such as the same author or the same descriptor or the same year of publication. A set is created by a computer when a searcher commands the computer to scan the database to retrieve all records that have the specified search term, for example, all records that include the word "Zaire."

social media/social networking: "Social media includes web-based and mobile based technologies which are used to turn communication into interactive dialogue between organizations, communities, and individuals. … Social media technologies take on many different forms including magazines, Internet forums, weblogs, social blogs, microblogging, wikis, podcasts, photographs or pictures, video, rating, and social bookmarking."

Examples of social media tools include Twitter, Facebook, LinkedIn, and YouTube. <http://en.wikipedia. org/wiki/Social_media>.

software: written computer programs that are used by the operating system of a computer. Examples of software include games, word processing programs and budgeting applications; also called programs or applications.

spam: "Spam is unsolicited or undesired bulk electronic messages. There is email spam, instant messaging spam, Usenet newsgroup spam, web search-engine spam, spam in blogs, and mobile phone-messaging spam. Spam includes legitimate advertisements, misleading advertisements, and phishing messages designed to trick recipients into giving up personal and financial information." McAffee, a company that sells virus protection software, provided this definition in its Virus Glossary at <http://home.mcafee.com/virusinfo>

stop words: "Words that are commonly used, like 'the,' 'a,' and 'for,' are usually ignored (these are called stop words). But there are even exceptions to this exception. The search [the who] likely refers to the band; the query [who] probably refers to the World Health Organization—Google will not ignore the word 'the' in the first query." These words are ignored because they tend to slow down your search without improving the results." *Google* Search Help. <http://support.google.com/websearch/bin/answer.py?hl=en&answer=136861>

subject heading: a search term used to describe the subject content of an information source; also called descriptor.

term: a word or multi-word phrase.

thesaurus: a list of terms used in a controlled vocabulary that shows relationships among them, such as broader terms, narrower terms, and related terms.

unbound periodical issue: an edition of a periodical that's part of a volume; for example, a quarterly edition of Ms. magazine is an unbound issue. In many libraries unbound issues of periodicals are shelved separately from their older volumes, which may be bound or kept in microformat.

URL: Uniform Resource Locator, an address on the World Wide Web.

usercode, username: the "name" used for one's computer account. The terms usercode and username are usually—but not always—interchangeable.

virus (also called a computer virus):   "A virus is a manmade program or piece of code that causes an unexpected, usually negative, event. Viruses are often disguised games or images with clever marketing titles such as "Me, nude." McAffee, a company that sells virus protection software, provided this definition in its Virus Glossary at <http://home.mcafee.com/virusinfo>.

website: any resource available on the World Wide Web. A website may simply refer you to information, or it may provide the full text of an article or research paper, a short video, or an excerpt from—or even a complete—sound recording. It may also be a short block of information about a person, an institution or a business, or a catalog from which you may order materials directly using a credit card. A website may have one page or many.

wireless: any communication that does not use wires to carry information. There are different techniques used in wireless communication including satellites, microwaves and radio. A term used often is **wi-fi,** which is short for wireless fidelity. The *Webopedia* <http://www.webopedia.com/TERM/w/ wireless.html> states: "In networking terminology, wireless is the term used to describe any computer network where there is no physical wired connection between sender and receiver, but rather the network is connected by radio waves and/or microwaves to maintain communications."

World Wide Web: a way to use the Internet. It's a protocol that links information in hypertext format.

References

Amazon.com. (2012, April 6). Privacy notice. Retrieved from http://www.amazon.com/gp/help/customer/display.html?nodeId5468496

American Civil Liberties Union. (n.d.). Technology and liberty. Retrieved from http://www.aclu.org/technology-and-liberty

American Heritage Dictionary of the English Language. (2000). (4th ed.). Boston, MA: Houghton Mifflin.

Apple.com. (2012). Internet glossary Macintosh OS. Retrieved from http://www.apple.com/quicktime/pdf/QT_Streaming_Server_v10.4.pdf

Bainwol, M. (2004, April 20). Illegal downloading. Letter to the editor. *New York Times.* Retrieved from http://www.nytimes.com/2004/04/24/opinion/l-illegal-downloading-339067.html

Brain, M. (1998–2012). Cookies. Retrieved from http://computer.howstuffworks.com/cookie1.htm

Bright Planet.com (2000–2012). Invisible web. Retrieved from http://websearch.about.com/od/invisibleweb/a/invisible_web.htm

Budapest open access initiative. (2002, February 14). Retrieved from http://www.soros.org/openaccess/read

Business Software Alliance. (2005, June 29). Educational efforts have spurred improvements since 2003 survey, but current attitudes and behaviors alarming. Retrieved from http://www.bsa.org/country/News%20and%20Events/News%20Archives/en/2005/en-06292005-collegedownloadsurvey.aspx

Encyclopedia Britannica Online. (2012). Subatomic particle: Classes of subatomic particles. Quarks and antiquarks. Retrieved from http://www.britannica.com/nobelprize/article-60740

Federal Trade Commission. (2011, March). Consumer sentinel network data book for January-December 2010. Retrieved from http://www.ftc.gov/sentinel/report/sentinel-annual-reports/sentinel-cy2010.pdf

Federal Trade Commission. (2011, March 8). FTC releases list of top consumer complaints in 2010; Identity theft tops the list again. Retrieved from ttp://ftc.gov/opa/2011/03/topcomplaints.shtm

Google.com. (2012). Stop words Google search help. Retrieved from http://support.google.com

Hurston, Z. (1942). *Dust tracks on a road.* Philadelphia, PA: Lippincott.

International Federation of Library Associations and Institutions (IFLA). (1999). Multilingual glossary for art librarians. Retrieved from http://archive.ifla.org/VII/s30/pub/mg1.htm#5

International Federation of Library Associations and Institutions (IFLA). (2005, August 2008). The Alexandria proclamation on information literacy and lifelong learning. Retrieved from http://archive.ifla.org/III/wsis/BeaconInfSoc.html

Kristol, D. M. (n.d.). Cookies & advertising networks technology brief. Retrieved from http://www.silicon-press.com/briefs/brief.cookiead/index.htm

McAffee.com. (2012). Virus glossary. Retrieved from http://home.mcafee.com/virusinfo

Merriam Webster Online Dictionary. (2012). Evaluate. Retrieved from http://www.merriam-webster.com/dictionary/evaluate

Milner Library, Illinois State University. (2012). Evaluating internet resources: Criteria to consider. Retrieved from http://ilstu.libguides.com/content.php?pid5121829

Milner Library, Illinois State University. (2012). Scholarship vs. propaganda. Retrieved from http://ilstu.libguides.com/content.php?pid5121829&sid51047964

Miniwatts Marketing Group. (2012). World internet usage statistics. Retrieved from http://www.internetworldstats.com/stats.htm

Mitchell, J. (n.d.). A reflection on media in the third world. Retrieved from http://www.medialit.org/reading-room/reflection-media-third-world

Moser, D. J. (2007). File sharing. Retrieved from http://www.copyrightguru.com/file_sharing_faq.htm

Oakland Community College. (2006–2008). Library tutorial on finding articles. Retrieved from http://oaklandcc.edu/library/searchpath/Module4/01c_journals.html

Organization for Economic Co-operation and Development. (2002, August 5). OECD glossary of statistical terms: Digital divide definition. Retrieved from http://stats.oecd.org/glossary/detail.asp?ID54719

Ponemon, L. (2004, December 28). Top 5 privacy issues for 2005. *ComputerWorld.* Retrieved from http://www.computerworld.com/s/article/98448/Top_5_privacy_issues_for_2005

Purdue University Online Writing Lab. (1995–2012). Paraphrase: Write it in your own words. Retrieved from http://owl.english.purdue.edu/owl/resource/619/01/

Reference and User Services Association. (2008). Using primary sources on the web. Retrieved from http://www.ala.org/rusa/resources/usingprimarysources#defining

Search Engine Watch. (2012). Retrieved from searchenginewatch.com

SearchNetworking.com (2004, February 22). DSL. Retrieved from http://searchwin2000.techtarget.com/sDefinition/0,,sid1_gci212964,00.html

TechTarget.com. (1999–2012). DSL. Retrieved from http://whatis.techtarget.com/reference/DSL-Glossary

Tehranian, J. (n.d.). Optimizing piracy: Achieving efficient management of intellectual property portfolios. Retrieved from http://www.onellp.com/parts/pubs/Tehranian_Optimizing_Piracy.pdf

U.S. Census Bureau. (2011). *Statistical abstract of the United States: 2012.* (131st ed.) Table 1155. p. 723. Washington, DC.

U.S. Copyright Office. (2006, July 12). Copyright and digital files. Retrieved from http://www.copyright.gov/help/faq/faq-digital.html

Webopedia.com. (2012). Retrieved from http://www.webopedia.com

WhatIs.com. (1999–2012). Server. Retrieved from http://whatis.techtarget.com/definition/0,,sid9_gci212964,00.html

Wikipedia, the free encyclopedia. (2012). Retrieved from http://en.wikipedia.org

WordNet Search 3.1. (n.d.). Retrieved from http://wordnetweb.princeton.edu/perl/webwn

YouTube.com. (2012, April 28). Copyright tips. Retrieved from http://www.youtube.com/t/howto_copyright

Young, H. (1983). *The ALA glossary of library and information science.* Chicago: ALA.

Index